Old school black moms got it right

DR. CALVIN AVANT

Copyright © 2024 by Dr. Calvin Avant.

ISBN: 978-1-7375082-6-7

All rights reserved. No part of this book may be reproduced, stored in a retrieval system, or transmitted in any form or by any means--electronic, mechanical, digital, photocopy, or any other without prior permission from the publisher and author, except as provided by the United States of America copyright law.

Unless otherwise noted, all scriptures are from the KING JAMES VERSION, public domain.

Scripture quotations marked (NIV) are taken from THE HOLY BIBLE, NEW INTERNATIONAL VERSION®. Copyright© 1973, 1978, 1984, 2011 by Biblica, Inc.™. Used by permission of Zondervan.

Scripture quotations marked (ESV) are taken from THE HOLY BIBLE, ENGLISH STANDARD VERSION®, Copyright© 2001 by Crossway, a publishing ministry of Good News Publishers. Used by permission.

Scripture quotations marked MSG are taken from THE MESSAGE, copyright © 1993, 2002, 2018 by Eugene H. Peterson. Used by permission of NavPress, represented by Tyndale House Publishers. All rights reserved.

Foreword

"It is easier to build strong children than to repair broken men."
Frederick Douglass

Everything I am, I owe to my mother's strength, courage, and wisdom. As a young black boy who grew up without a positive or consistent presence from my father, one of the most outstanding things that my mother did for me when I was growing up was to make sure that I was exposed to, and had access to, positive black men. Just as important, she instilled enough fear in me early enough that I never questioned her as the head of the household or dared challenge her. This healthy fear was grounded in love, and I know that because she told me so. My mother knew from the moment I was born, the world that awaited me as a black man, and everything she did for me, every lesson, was to prepare me for the world I would walk into as a man.

When I was seven years old, my mother and I shared a traumatic experience that showed me how fearless my mother was when it came to protecting my sister and I. I was outside bouncing a tennis ball off the side of the building, and before I knew it, the Jump Out Squad (a notorious police narcotics division in the 1980's) ran up, guns blazing and dogs barking, demanding everyone get on the ground. I had seen this several times when I lived in DC, so I stood, ball in hand, amused and smiling. Then the officer pointed his gun directly at me and forcefully told me to get on the ground.

Curious and confused, I pointed to myself, and the officer shouted, "Yes! You!" It was at this point that the gravity of the situation came into view. I laid down on the concrete, belly and face down, and extended my arms and hands forward away from my body, just like all the other black men on the ground. Not 10 seconds later, my mother came running out of the building and grabbed me off the ground with one hand. She turned to the police and proceeded to curse and shame every officer present. She took me inside, and despite living paycheck to paycheck, she found a way to move us to Silver Spring, MD, not one week later. That was my mother. She was not a superhuman being, however, she was fiercely protective and never afraid to make the necessary changes to keep my sister and I out of harm's way.

Forty (40) years later, I have a crystal-clear understanding of why my mother raised me the way she did, and I have a deeper appreciation for my mother's courage and conviction in making decisions to protect my sister and I. Regardless of our financial situation, she focused on building our character. Had she allowed me to slack off in school or run the streets with friends (and some family members) involved in the drug game; had she allowed me to keep my stash of stolen Matchbox cars versus making me take them back and apologize to the store manager, I would not be the man that I am today. My character and integrity are what I am most proud of, and I owe 50% of that to my mother. I owe the other 50% to my mentor since 1987 and the author of this book, Dr. Calvin Avant.

Dr. Calvin Avant is unequivocally the most honest person I've ever met. When he loves you and wants the best for you, he will unapologetically tell you the truth about you, to your face. He's not mean about it; he is firm, and he is fair. In a world where people are afraid to speak their truth for fear of being canceled, this type of honesty, while jaw-dropping and shocking at times, is exactly what we need to fix what is broken in our community. He is a straight shooter with compassion.

When it comes to the plight of the black boy and black man in America, there are so many contributing factors that it is hard to know where to begin to solve the problem. It is now common knowledge that systemic racism is at the root of almost every problem black males face (i.e., broken families, academic achievement gap, unemployment, mass incarceration, police brutality), but knowing that will not fix the problem. This book is not about how we got to this point; It's about how to move forward.

The modern-day criminal justice system feeds on the souls of black folks by way of mass incarceration. For us to starve this system of its favorite meal, we must train our children from birth on how to combat this system. We want our young people to not just survive, but thrive. While making this a reality will take the entire village to raise the child, that child's parent is their first and most impactful teacher. There is a Ghanaian proverb that states: "The ruin of a nation begins in the homes of its people." If the ruin of a nation begins there, so shall the healing.

Dr. Avant has constantly and consistently reminded me that I owe my survival and my success to my mother's "take no crap" approach to raising me. My father made minimal contributions to my growth and development, but my mother's tenacity in protecting my sister and I from failure (academic and moral) more than made up for his absence. My respect for elders, my respect for women, and my understanding of the importance of education all come from how my mother raised me. These lessons were not optional; they were required as a part of my ability to stay under my mother's roof, eat her food, and get clothes as needed. These were the conditions of our parent-child partnership.

I use the term parent-child partnership because while my mother was the unopposed captain of the ship, she gave enough leeway for my sister and I to grow into our personalities, encouraged us to be explorers, and simultaneously served as our bumper guard (think kiddie bowling) to ensure we did not end up in the gutter. Only when I had shown my mother that I could behave responsibly and be trusted did she make room for me to make my own decisions. My mother gave me plenty of space to grow and learn, but as long as we were under her roof, she was the final decider. She loved us too much to let us screw up.

I believe this partnership is missing from many mother/son relationships today. My mother created a code of conduct that outlined language and behavior that was allowable and, more importantly, what was not allowable. She also let me know when I could have fun (usually with family and neighbors), and when I needed to behave and "act like you got some home training!" (usually with her co-workers and church folk). She let me know what the consequences were if I went outside of the code. This included lightning smacks, discrete jabs to the chest, and clinched teeth under the breath promises of butt whippings when we got home. Talk about a long car ride home.

Today, parents in the United States negotiate with their children from early ages. Many parents today treat their children as friends or equals. From a developmental perspective, I think this is a very dangerous practice. The latest research shows that human brains don't fully develop until between 21 and 25 years of age. Giving young people, especially young people who have not even begun their journey through puberty (a major hormonal milestone in child development), the ability to make life-altering decisions while they are still changing biologically has a very high risk attached to it. Even during the teen and late teen years, the risk associated with adolescent decision-making remains high. Who amongst us hasn't acted out in rebellion when we were young only to laugh at ourselves later in life about how much we thought we knew? Thank goodness we didn't kill ourselves.

Thanks to the introduction of social media, many traditional values, such as respect for elders, are no longer a given. There are distractions and debates about what should be done everywhere, yet the problem seems to be getting worse. In 2006, Erik Eckholm of the New York Times reported, "In response to the worsening situation for young black men, a growing number of programs are placing as much importance on teaching life skills -- like parenting, conflict resolution, and character building -- as they are on teaching job skills." For generations, these life skills were learned at home; what happened?

How we raise our boys into men has never been more important. Violence amongst our youth has skyrocketed in recent years, so making sure our boys and young men know how to handle themselves (i.e., de-escalation vs. escalation of a situation) is a must. This is where the knowledge, wisdom, and experience of Dr. Calvin Avant comes in. Dr. Avant has dedicated his life to helping black men not only survive, but thrive! A father, a pastor, a mentor, a coach, a community leader, and a sincere service leader at all times,

Dr. Avant delivers truth unfiltered. He is not concerned with coddling individuals and their feelings; he is concerned with getting to the root of problems and solving them.

When reading this book, you will no doubt feel like Dr. Avant is pointing his finger in your face and challenging you directly, and that is exactly the intent. There are enough books out today that throw a lot of words at the problems our young black boys and men face today. This book gives an action plan, and that action plan begins in the home. The journey of a thousand miles begins with a single step; this book is that first step.

Larry Meadow Jr. MBA

Contents

Why Me?.. i

CHAPTER 1 – FATHERLESS BOYS 1
Fatherless 2
Deadbeat Dads 6

CHAPTER 2 – WAYS NEW SCHOOL BLACK MOMS RUIN BOYS 9
Ways New School Black Moms Ruin Boys 10
Speaking Negatively About Their Father and Other Men.....................13
The Missing Boundaries and Coping Skills Needed for Success 16

CHAPTER 3 – NIPPING IT IN THE BUD..20
Discipline Does Not Start at the Point of an Incident 21
Inconsistent Discipline 23
You Are Not Your Child's Friend 25

CHAPTER 4 – EMOTIONAL INCEST & OUT-DIRECTED NEGATIVE EMOTIONS 27
Emotional Incest 28
Outer-Directed Negative Emotions 34

CHAPTER 5 – "THE TALK"..39
The Talk: A Generational Practice 40
How Mainstream America Views Black Boys as a Threat.....................42
How "The Talk" Lead to Books, Documentaries, and Television Shows 45
When Should Black Boys Receive the Talk? 46
The Dos and Don'ts when Black Boys Deal with the Police 50

CHAPTER 6 – BLACK BOYS IN A SELF CRISIS 59
Black Boys in a Self Crisis 60
Steps to Addressing the Self Crisis 64
Developing a Positive Self-Image 67
Black Boys with Poor Self-Esteem 72
Develop Positive Self-Esteem in Black Boys..82
Black Boys Lacking Self-Discipline 89
Respect Yourself 96
Black Boys Self-Fulfillment of Dreams (Self-Realization)....................101

CHAPTER 7 – OLD SCHOOL BLACK MOMS GOT IT RIGHT 117
    Old School Black Moms Got it Right 118
    New School Black Mom Toolbox for Raising Black Boys 123
    Old School Black Moms Came with a Bible and a Belt 129
    The Bible 131
    The Belt 142
    It Takes a Village to Raise a Child 145
About the Author 151
References 153

WHY ME?

You may ask what would give me the qualifications to express my views on this subject. I have worked with an at-risk youth population, especially with Black Boys, for the past 45 years. I have worked in a recreational setting located across the street from a public housing project. I have directed and counseled runaways, homeless, battered, abused, and neglected boys in shelter care. I have taught in a title one elementary school. I was an instructor in at-risk self-contained behavior modification classes for middle and high school students. I have taught in high school abeyance programs. I have also coached middle and high school boys' basketball. I have authored a social skills curriculum and conducted classes from it for elementary and at-risk charter high schools. I was a Youth Outreach Worker in Washington, DC redirecting at-risk teen boys from delinquent behavior. I have instructed behavior modification courses for juveniles who have been adjudicated as adults who have committed major crimes up to and including murder. I have authored a parenting manual for at-risk children entitled, "So You Are Raising a Knuckle Head." This curriculum has been used for over 20 years teaching inmates in county jails and state prisons. I have directed state-funded diversion programs for first-time offenders coming into the juvenile justice system. I was both a Chaplain, and a Substance Abuse Clinical Director in a state prison system. And finally, I was the director of a substance abuse program in Washington, DC. Because of my extensive work history, I have acquired a wealth of knowledge and have a clear understanding of Black Boys and why they miss the mark and do not become productive citizens. Additionally, I understand the skills they lack due to growing up without a father or a positive male role model in their lives. The skills that they lack include, but are not exclusive to the following:

- a lack of morals, values, and ethics,
- a lack of self-worth, poor decision making,
- a lack of self-discipline,
- an understanding of choices and consequences,
- and a need for education

In my 45-year career of working with Black Boys and their parents through training, research, observation, and discussions, I have discovered a sharp decline of morals, values, and ethics in many Black Boys. Again, the main factors that have contributed to this chaotic state in the lives of Black Boys continue to be a lack of a father in the home and positive male role models in their lives. Without these positive male role models, it has created an atmosphere that pulls many Black Boys to a life of crime, corruption, violence, substance abuse, dropping out of high school, and engaging in risky sexual behavior. This causes a dysfunctional lifestyle and hinders them from becoming productive citizens.

Over the past 25 years, the one constant factor I was able to discern was boys need positive men in their lives if they are to grow up and become hardworking and successful men. This positive male attention should come first from their fathers. But the old school method of the village helping to raise the child can also be very supportive. There is no shortage of knowledgeable experts — psychologists or family therapists — who have discussed how father-absence impacted Black Boys' productivity in life as well as the mental health of many of these Boys. I truly believe to turn the tide and change this behavior, we need a community of males who are willing to mentor Black Boys. Not only do we need assistance from these Black men to change this destructive behavior, but we need the village to raise the child. This village includes present fathers, mothers, brothers, sisters, aunts, teachers, coaches, and preachers. I am saying all hands on deck to raise healthy and successful Black Boys.

CHAPTER 1

FATHERLESS BOYS

HAVING A FATHER OR A POSTIVE MALE ROLE MODEL IS THE REMEDY FOR THE CHAOS IN THE LIVES OF THESE BOYS

FATHERLESS

Rod Liddle was branded a "national disgrace" when he wrote about how Black Boys are paying the price for growing up in households without their dads. But he was and still is right. The disproportionate number of Black Boys held in county jails adjudicated as adults is ghastly. Studies have shown that youths in father-absent households have the highest odds of being incarcerated and higher levels of behavioral problems in schools and are more likely to be suspended from school (Williams, 2014). Research by Princeton University sociology professor Sara McLanahan notes that a father's absence increases anti-social behavior (McLanahan & Jencks, 2015). This results in drug use and reduces a child's chances of gainful, legitimate, and legal employment. In the report "Growing Up Without Father: The Effects on African American Boys," Cory Ellis found that father-absence was the strongest indicator of delinquency, even more so than low socioeconomic status or peer pressure (Ellis, 2009). There is also evidence that fatherless children have lower self-esteem and a greater risk for mental illness, suicide, and risk of depression.

I taught behavior modification classes at a county jail where I discussed the issue of growing up fatherless openly with the young men. Many of those young men had been involved in violent crimes. So, what was going wrong? I cut to the chase and asked what were the main issues that caused them to get into so much trouble. Nearly all the issues pointed to the absence of their fathers as a key problem in their lives. The participants stated that they were simply left to fend for themselves. They also said they learned to become a man from their peers and guys on the streets. Their lessons on how to treat women were from listening to rappers and guys who had a side piece, who were abusive or deadbeat dads. These young men had not been taught the concept of morals, values, ethics, or anger management. Many did not understand how these concepts could help them to have a successful life. Tupac Shakur, the late rapper, once said: "But I know for a fact that if I had a father, I'd have some discipline. I'd have more confidence. Your mother cannot calm you down the way a man can. Your mother can't reassure you the way a man can. My mother couldn't show me where my manhood was. You need a man to teach you how to be a man." He admitted he began running with gangs because he wanted the things a father gives to a child; structure and protection.

Some of the boys in the class had little remorse or did not feel responsible for their crimes. Others maintained that they had done some of the things but would not confess to all the charges. Very few accepted the blame for their criminal behavior. Evidence shows that Black Boys are more likely to plead not guilty to crimes than their white counterparts (Fouzder, 2016). Inevitably, this leads to longer sentences when they are found guilty. So, what was the reason for this state of denial among these young men? Their response often had to do with respect. "I felt justified killing him," "the argument went left," "because he disrespected me." For many of them, these excuses made all the sense in the world. This is because many of these boys are raised without a father who could teach them the morals and values needed to see what was wrong with this behavior. Many of these boys resort to the streets to get their answers. This is where this mindset starts; this population is left to learn from others who do not have the necessary social skills and are living unproductive lives. President Obama cited the need for fathers to realize that responsibility doesn't just end at conception; "That doesn't make you a father. What makes you a father is not the ability to have a child. Any fool can have a child. It's the courage to raise a child that makes you a father."

He also commented about the burden that single parenthood was on his mother, who raised him with the help of his maternal grandparents. "I know the toll it took on me, not having a father in the house," he continued. "The hole in your heart when you don't have a male figure in the home who can guide you and lead you."

Black mothers are put in tough positions when Black men help create a life, especially boys, then refuse to help them raise these boys to grow up to become men. In addition to not being physically present, many fathers never give the mother money for their children, placing even more responsibility on the single mothers. Many Black Moms often have guilt associated with being a single black mom, being no fault of her own. Single Black Moms often find themselves paralyzed with guilt because they don't have the support of their child's father.

DEADBEAT DADS

Before I start my discourse on how new school Black Moms have missed the mark in raising Black Boys, I must be real and explain why. First, it is important that we look at the structure of the Black Family. The Black Family has been in a free fall. From a Pew Research Center analysis of U.S. Census Bureau data, more than half (58%) of black children are living with an unmarried parent; 47% with a single mom; 30% of single mothers and their families are living in poverty compared with 17% of single fathers and their families and 16% of families headed by cohabitating couples. In comparison, 8% of married couple families are living below the poverty line (Livingston, 2018). Black mothers that I know personally face a daunting task as they are entangled in the day-to-day difficulties of plotting a course living as a Black Woman and rearing Black Boys, all while in the presence of many societal issues is. As the sole parent in the household, Black Mothers are left with the task of continuously empowering and encouraging their sons to become positive, productive Black Men despite the reality that in America, Black Boys are often considered threats or thugs rather than students, sons, fathers, brothers, or even humans. Many Black Mothers are in a painful situation, knowing that we are still living in a country without equality and justice for their sons. There are also many Black Moms who do not have the skill set to navigate through these treacherous and perilous times for Black Boys.

Without help rearing these boys, they make many mistakes, causing many of them to exhibit dysfunctional behavior throughout their lives. These moms are in a unique position because of their social and racial circumstances, as well as not having the child's father there to help. Many of these moms suffer from high-stress levels while providing for the family, which influences everything they do as parents. Increasing experience to life's pressures, connected with restricted access to income, can make things worse, such as mental strain or tension related to the role of being a parent. This elevated financial uncertainty causes preoccupation in acquiring the funds needed for the family; the growth and development of the child must take a back seat and are not a high priority.

Many Black families have had to endure the lack of fathers in the home to help guide, protect, and support them. This absentee father is commonly referred to as a deadbeat dad who is a man who intentionally doesn't take care of their children physically, mentally, emotionally, or financially. Many of these deadbeat dads are poor role models, owe child support, or just walk off, leaving the family high and dry and not caring if the family lives or dies. These so-called men see themselves as baby making machines and believe their jobs are done at the point of conception. These deadbeat dads are a major reason African American communities grapple with the school-to-prison pipeline, teen fathers, gun violence, high unemployment and mass incarceration of young black men. It is this author's belief that the main factor contributing to this chaotic state in the lives of Black Boys continues to be a lack of a father in the home. The lack of a male role model has created a life of crime, corruption, violence, substance abuse, high school dropouts, and risky sexual behavior; in other words, a dysfunctional lifestyle in the lives of many Black Boys. They live a life, unlike their peers who live with both parents who are married, which has caused many Black Boys not to become positive productive citizens and fail in life.

CHAPTER 2

WAYS NEW SCHOOL BLACK MOMS RUIN BOYS

"YOU'RE JUST LIKE YOUR NO-GOOD DADDY"

WAYS NEW SCHOOL BLACK MOMS RUIN BOYS

One of the most toxic environments a Black Boy can grow up in is living without a father or a positive Black male role model. Contrary to the belief of most feminists and liberals, a woman CANNOT be a mother and a father to a boy. Nor can she raise a boy to become a man without help from positive males. A mother cannot be a mother and a father, too. No matter how great a mother she is, she can never be a father. Many mistakes will be made while a single mother tries to teach her son how to become a man. Mistakes that often put their sons on the wrong path in life. These mistakes occur because she does not understand how a male would handle many situations during her son's growth toward manhood. This can create a lost, confused young man, resulting in self-crisis. The self-crisis includes poor self-image, lack of self-discipline, low self-esteem, and lack of self-respect. We will discuss this self-crisis in its entirety in Chapter 5.

Some Black Moms deliberately and purposely devise a plan to corrupt their sons' minds against their fathers. Some moms do it inadvertently. Because of the mom's conduct, the boy can grow up having extreme resentment toward his father. Many boys display this resentment by becoming very disobedient, joining gangs, and getting involved in the juvenile and adult justice systems. The boys become substance abusers, becoming very violent as well, and they also find themselves involved in unhealthy sexual relationships. The mother's behavior can also cause the boy to develop self-hatred and to remember that when he looks internally, he'll see himself being just like the father because he is a part of him.

Some of these moms project a romantic relationship onto their son as if she is using him to fill a void in her own life. This is not a sexual relationship, but an emotional relationship. You can refer to this as "Emotional Incest." This kind of behavior can be debilitating to boys during their growth and maturity period. The boy is put under undue stress when he is expected to take on the role of a missing mate. It may sound far-fetched, but many mothers do this to their sons, often without recognizing it. Many single mothers hate their son's girlfriends because they fear that as he gets closer to this female, he'll start establishing healthy boundaries that will separate the emotional ties they have with each other. These mothers often have no idea the shortcomings they are causing in their son's life. This behavior can have an overwhelming influence on the boys' psyche. One must remember that the principles, beliefs, and standards learned as boys become the principles, beliefs, and standards used as a man to resolve the challenges he will face as an adult. We will discuss the subject in depth in chapter 4.

Boys need a relationship with their father and/or other positive males to gain a sense of themselves and their male identity. Without these relationships, they often grow up lost and confused about what a man is. The mom should NEVER deny the father a right to see his child. When boys can't answer those questions that only a father can answer, they take cues from the media, their moms, their peers, and men in the street to fill in the empty space regarding what type of man they should become. It is important to remember that the morals, values, and ethics taught as a boy becomes a man are the same ones he will use to resolve life's problems as an adult.

SPEAKING NEGATIVELY ABOUT THEIR FATHER AND OTHER MEN

One of the most toxic environments a boy can grow up in is living without a father. A mother cannot be a mother and a father. No matter how great a mother she is, she can never be a father. Many mistakes will be made while a single mother is trying to teach her son how to become a man. Often moms are placed in unfamiliar circumstances and even if her intentions are good, she can still lead her son down the wrong path. This happens because she does not understand how a male would handle many situations that occur during her son's growth toward manhood.

ATTEMPT BY A MOTHER TO DISTANCE HER SON FROM THE FATHER

The deliberate attempt by a mother to distance her son from the father is known as Parental Alienation Syndrome (Meyer, 2018). Distancing father and son is used to destroy the parental connection between the boy and the father. Moms often try to alienate the boy from the father using tactics. For instance, forcing the boy to choose between parents, telling the boy the other parent does not love them, giving the child the impression that the father is somehow dangerous. Other examples may include requesting that the boy spy on the father, lying on the father about sexual, physical or emotional abuse, or giving the boy details about ongoing conflict between her and the father. The mother may also discuss financial problems brought on by the father not being in the home, telling the boy about legal issues between her and the father, or saying horrible things about the father openly to the boy. This can create a lost and confused young man, resulting in a self-crisis. This includes poor self-image, lack of self-discipline, low self-esteem or no self-respect. We will discuss this self-crisis in its entirety in Chapter 5. The sad reality is that when the mother damages their son's natural affection for the father, they inflict serious — and even abusive — harm on the boy.

Contrary to the belief of most feminists and liberals, a woman CANNOT be a mother and a father to a boy. Nor can she raise a boy to become a man without help from positive males. Boys need that relationship with their father supported by other positive male authority figures to gain a sense of themselves. Positive male role models are necessary for boys to understand their masculinity and male identity. Without these relationships, they often grow up lost and confused about their identity as a man. While things between a single mother and the child's father may have gone to the left, the mother should NEVER deny the father a right to see his child if he wants to see them. When pointed in the wrong direction as to what a man should look like, they take signals from hypermasculine images in the media, ideas from their peers, or men in their environment to fill in the empty space regarding what type of man they should become. And if this media isn't available, he starts taking cues from his mother regarding what type of man he should be.

<u>PROJECTING ANGER AIMED AT THE FATHER ONTO THE SON</u>

It is not unusual for a single mother to go into an angry rant when her son does something wrong, makes a mistake, or when he disagrees with her. Oftentimes, she is venting the rage she feels about the child's father towards the son. A common statement is, "You are going to grow up to be just like your no-good daddy." Sometimes, she will even hit the boy with her fist. Frequently, these emotionally abusive acts knock boys down for the count emotionally before they even have an opportunity to rise to manhood. God forbid her son looks like the father. Every time she looks at the child, she does not see the kid; she sees the father and can become abusive toward the child. Many times, punishing him for the smallest thing he has done. These hostile and negative statements from a single mother can force boys to withdraw socially and erect emotional walls. These walls can prevent boys from connecting with others and forming healthy relationships when they get older.

THE MISSING BOUNDARIES AND COPING SKILLS NEEDED FOR SUCCESS

BOUNDARIES

Some Single Black Mother's idea of structure is totally different than how men see it. Most men understand structure must include establishing healthy boundaries. Boundaries are imaginary lines in the sand that keep boys safe. Those imaginary lines keep boys from going too far and doing things that will hurt them. A strong father teaches their son what boundaries are at an early age.

Boys who grow up without boundaries cross lines. They take dangerous, unnecessary risks. They don't know when they have gone too far. They violate people's personal space. They also cannot take NO for an answer. This leads to people having to take extensive measures, such as filing restraining orders or having them arrested. They are beaten severely, or they may even be killed to get them to stop whatever they are doing.

COPING SKILLS

When a father or positive male influence is absent, instruction on coping skills for boys is commonly lacking. Boys who grow up in single-parent homes often do not learn how to cope with the problems that come with evolving into manhood. When they face failure, rejection, death, hurt, and pain, they do not know how to handle the situation. These instances create boys who deal with things from an emotional viewpoint rather than thinking logically about how to handle situations. Many times, they do not go through the grieving process and hold on to many of these experiences throughout their lives, thus stunting their growth into manhood.

Black Boys who have not been taught coping skills by their fathers make irrational decisions. When life throws a curve ball at them, they react inappropriately. If someone is pregnant, they say it's not their child. Life gets hard; they walk off and leave their family. When they lose a job, they become a deadbeat dad. Ron Mincy of Columbia University's School of Social Work stated, "a father sets boundaries — discipline and training. Mincy points out, a father provides a sense of protection. Boys without fathers lack the paternal support they need to respond to the things that life brings them. There are certain questions a boy would never ask a female, he says. "At some point in their life, every man is vulnerable," Mincy explains. "You have circumstances in your life that you need to be able to go to a man to debrief. So, it's this insecurity, it's that fear, it's that absence of someone who loves me, who cares about me and I can go and I can ask anything" (Joiner, 2016).

Psychologist Fred Phillips, senior adviser, and psychologist at the Progressive Life Center, a Washington, D.C. points out, how does a developing young man learn how to be in healthy relationships and balance the emotions of tenderness and assertiveness? Without guidance and direction, young men will more than likely ignore, sabotage, or deny their emotions. They don't know what to do with them in the context of this environment, which has a certain image of males. If it's not directed, if it's not shaped, then [this energy] gets out of control, and that's what we see. That's the critical piece. Emotions are energy. Emotions are biochemical, and they're electricity. That energy, whether it is pain, whether it's hurt, whether it's anger, has to go somewhere." Phillips notes that when an adolescent acts out, it's usually a form of communication. They are expressing their pain, he explains. That's why school systems are bringing in more social workers and therapists to help educators address students' emotional needs (Joiner, 2016).

Wizdom Powell, associate professor of health behavior at the University of North Carolina's Gillings School of Global Public Health said "boys are watching the way that men relate to other people who are important to them, and they're picking up on cues on how to form healthy functional relationships with another human being. They're also learning messages about masculinity and manhood that mothers can also provide, but through a different kind of lens" (Joiner, 2016).

Powell says boys are learning the social rules around masculinity, manhood, and how men in their lives, particularly their fathers, either respond to or accept those rules. They also observe how they push back on them to modify and create new forms, or ways, of being men in the world. "And while women can talk about that, and can try to impart that kind of knowledge to boys, they're not living it in the same way that men are. The opportunities for modeling that kind of behavior are limited for women, because we can't model for boys how to look, to be, and act, and function in the world as a man. There are many parts of the developmental process that I think women can't be stand-ins for," Powell says. "We can help boys negotiate rules around masculinity more effectively, but we can't model them in the same way that men can model them for their sons, and also for their daughters" (Joiner, 2016).

CHAPTER 3

NIPPING IT IN THE BUD

YOU SHOULD STOP NEGATIVE BEHAVIOR WHEN IT FIRST APPEARS. THIS IS WHEN IT IS AT ITS WEAKEST POINT.
NIP - NIP - NIP - NIP!

DISCIPLINE DOES NOT START AT THE POINT OF AN INCIDENT

The word discipline means to impart knowledge and skill – to teach. However, it is normally associated with punishment and control. There is a great deal of controversy about the appropriate ways to discipline children; parents are often confused about effective ways to set limits and instill self-control in their children.

The problem with discipline is moms often focus on the obedience part and forget the training part. Moms with Black Boys must understand that if you want your teenage son to behave in a certain manner, they must be trained to do so before the teenage years arrive. My Grandma Amy Thomas, born in 1890, who could not read or write, gave me some great advice concerning discipline and children. She said, "I'm going to give you two acorns; I want you to plant each of them and allow them to grow. Allow the first one to grow for 10 months and the second for 10 years. At the end of each period, go back and pull the plant out of the ground. You can easily wrap your hand around the one with

10 months of growth and pull it out of the ground. But the one with 10 years of growth will require a block and tackle to pull it out of the ground." She was trying to explain that behavior is much like those plants; once the behavior is rooted and grounded it is very difficult to remove it from someone.

That means if you want your son to be respectful to all adults and have good morals and ethics, they will have to practice these behaviors early and consistently during their growth toward manhood. Training is done every day and every hour that you spend with your son. You must get into the trenches with him. Many moms do not want to get dirty. However, it takes getting a bit dirty to understand all the things a boy will go through.

INCONSISTENT DISCIPLINE

Along with coddling, the most damaging thing single Black Mothers do to their sons is enforce inconsistent discipline. Because they do not understand the role a father plays in establishing consistent structure and order in a child's life, they either do not punish boys for their bad behavior or they go overboard with excessively violent or harsh punishments.

Many moms phrase the question, "isn't that cute?" Moms also state, "he's just going through a phase." **It's not cute, and they are not just going through a phase; it's learned behavior.** Both comments are used when the child is doing something that is not suitable for their age or against societal norms. The parent cannot use these labels to excuse or explain gateway behaviors to delinquency.

When moms use emotions to make decisions concerning their son's bad behavior, many times, they do not have a plan of action to correct the bad behavior or to educate them that what they are doing is wrong. Without any positive direction, this bad behavior frequently persists well into manhood. This reaction from mom occurs because when disciplining her son, mom does not recognize Newton's third law: For every action, there is an equal and opposite reaction. In other words, if you allow the child's negative behavior to continue, you can always expect detrimental consequences in return. Therefore, many of them get arrested for selling drugs and cannot wait to get out of jail and get back to work hustling on the streets.

YOU ARE NOT YOUR CHILD'S FRIEND

If a mother loves her son emotionally but neglects the functional role, that boy is at risk of not maturing into a responsible adult. Indeed, emotional, and functional parenting roles go hand-in-hand. It's not healthy to emphasize one at the cost of the other. You need both (Lehman).

Moms also need to understand that the amount of emotional versus functional requirements changes over time. As a child gets older, the parent needs to take on more of a functional role and less of an emotional role because the goal for older kids is to prepare them to live life without you. And because many moms continue to discipline with emotions, their boys do not learn the rules necessary to understand what life expects of them.

Understand that your child can find another friend, but your child cannot find another mother. You, and only you can be your child's mother, and that's why you need to be the parent and not the friend.

A mom who desires to have a friendship with her son is incapable of delivering effective discipline. Discipline, if it is properly corrective, does not always make the son feel warm and fuzzy toward the parent. If a mom thinks her son's teachers are in error, she should keep it to herself and deal with the school directly. Be careful what you say to your son about it and be mindful of any displeasure you may show towards his teacher's actions. If the parent undermines what the teacher is saying in the classroom, the child may become uncooperative with the teacher due to a lack of respect because of what the mother has said.

At the end of the day, the son needs to be able to have relationships that are separate from their relationship with their mom. Dependency – where the mom or their son become dependent on one another for friendship, can backfire. If there is a disagreement or a conflict, that friendship and the mother-son relationship can be destroyed.

CHAPTER 4

EMOTIONAL INCEST & OUTER-DIRECTED NEGATIVE EMOTIONS

EMOTIONAL INCEST IS NOT SEXUAL BEHAVIOR. INSTEAD, THIS UNHEALTHY BEHAVIOR IS WHERE THE MOTHER SEEKS EMOTIONAL SUPPORT FROM HER SON THAT SHOULD BE SOUGHT FROM AN ADULT RELATIONSHIP

EMOTIONAL INCEST

A Black Boy who grows up in single-parent home often does not learn how to control his emotions. When they do not have a means of self-controlling their emotions, it can lead to the inability to cope with many of life's struggles. As a Black Boy grows up, he must have restraint to work his way through living in this world while being Black in America. He must be raised to think first logically and then add his emotions to the equation. When he uses logical thinking first to reason, it usually causes him to develop self-control over his emotions, which can aid him in making better decisions. When the boy thinks logically, he thinks critically and objectively utilizing the concept that choices have consequences.

I am not saying that the behavior titled "Emotional Incest" is limited to single Black Moms or that this behavior is more likely to appear in homes in Black communities. However, I will say that many times this behavior can be found in economically deprived communities where personal boundaries are unclear and emotional incest is often seen as ordinary.

Emotional incest is when a mother uses a child for emotional support in a way that is normal for a husband or boyfriend (blackleaderanalysis, 2016). Specifically, these are single mothers who project a romantic relationship onto their sons as if they are using them to fill a void in their own lives. Emotional incest is sexual energy without touching that can include inappropriate affection or sexual talk, coming into the bathroom, etc. Emotional incest occurs when a child feels responsible for a parent's emotional well-being. It occurs because the parents are emotionally dishonest with themselves and cannot get their emotional needs met by other adults. John Bradshaw refers to this dynamic as a parent making the child their a "surrogate spouse" (Burney). Emotional incest that occurs during childhood or adolescence can lead to intimacy disorders, sexual addiction, relationship problems and emotional distancing (The Right Step, 2017). Trust and closeness issues can drive fear of intimacy, leaving the boy feeling overwhelmed and overly responsible even early on in a relationship. Some boys/men prefer fleeting or even anonymous sexual encounters versus the "baggage" that comes with a relationship due to their issues with intimacy.

A Black Woman who does not have a romantic companion, lacks an emotional outlet or financial support to help her. This lack of support leads to searching for support from sources that are unhealthy. One of the ways emotional incest can appear is by a mother telling her son about parts of her romantic escapades. However, the most common way emotional incest happens is by berating and insulting a boy's father in front of him. A boy sees himself as his father, and an insult to his father is the same or worse than abusing the boy. Also, if a boy loses respect for his father, he will have no role model for his development. The boy will not be grounded in anything. The media's perception of a black man will have complete control of the son. Diminishing a boy's image of his father can destroy a boy's core self-esteem (blackleaderanalysis, 2016).

Using a son as an emotional sounding board is another form of emotional incest. A woman should not talk to a son about how hard it is to find a man and details of why her past relationships did not work. A son does not need to know if his mother is insecure about her body or if the mother is uncomfortable around men for any reason. A son should not be made aware of the intimate details concerning the mother's dating life (blackleaderanalysis, 2016).

Financial emotional incest is when a son is required or expected to give money to the mother to pay bills. Again, supplementing the household budget is the job of a husband or boyfriend (blackleaderanalysis, 2016). Financial emotional incest is not a child working to buy his things like schoolbooks, field trip tickets, or sports equipment. Requiring a child that is not eighteen years old to pitch in to make sure the household budget is met, reinforces the idea that intimacy is dependent on financial support. Coupling intimacy and financial support will cause dysfunction in the child's future dating life.

A son's need to financially support a mother is a paradigm more prevalent in the black community than the white community. Most black athletes in interviews talk about how they were able to buy their mother a house (blackleaderanalysis, 2016). Some Black Boys caught up in financial emotional incest will resort to making money in the streets. They may sell drugs, steal, rob, or employ other illegal behaviors to bring home the bacon. A son will feel that his essential manhood will be in question if he fails to help his mother. His core self-esteem is linked to providing financial support for the family due to the concept of financial emotional incest.

HOW A MOTHER CAN AVOID EMOTIONAL INCEST WITH HER SON?

Some of the ways to avoid emotional incest may include starting with family pre-planning, having same-sex friendships, and relationships and proper money management. Same-sex friendships and relationships are the most important of all. If a person has friends of the same sex, they can vent in a healthy manner. People with numerous same-sex friendships are more likely to have better romantic relationships because they are not expecting the romantic partner to fulfill them totally (blackleaderanalysis, 2016). A large part of having a healthy relationship is setting realistic expectations and boundaries (blackleaderanalysis, 2016). This practice will assist the mother in not relying on her son for emotional fulfillment.

The less obvious method to prevent emotional incest is to evaluate the criticisms from their children. When children are growing up, they will make many unreasonable requests or get emotional when they do not get what they want. Children's unreasonable requests cause parents to write off whatever their children say as irrational. If a child is expressing anger toward you for being emotionally draining, listen with compassion. Often, mothers attack their sons when they criticize them. Normally, the mother accuses the son of being ungrateful or says hurtful things like, "You are just like your no-good daddy!" The mother then lists everything she has ever done for her son and reminds him of all his failures. If a son's frustration is not validated, the son will grow up to repress his negative emotions around women. The repression of emotion will lead to horrible relationship dynamics in a child's future (blackleaderanalysis, 2016).

Many single mothers hate their sons having girlfriends because they fear that as they get closer to this female, they will start establishing healthy boundaries that will separate their emotional tie. These mothers often have no idea of the destruction they are causing in their sons' life. This type of behavior has an overwhelming influence on the male child's psyche. One must remember that the morals, values, and ethics taught as boys become the morals, values, and ethics he will use as a man to resolve the challenges he will face in life as an adult.

OUTER-DIRECTED NEGATIVE EMOTIONS

It is my opinion that a woman **CANNOT** be a mother and a father to a boy. Nor can she successfully raise a boy to become a man all by herself. A boy needs a relationship with his father or other positive men to gain a sense of himself. Without that relationship, they often grow up lost and confused about their identity as a man. This confusion is sometimes caused by some moms using outer-directed negative emotions when disciplining or punishing the boy. I have observed over the past 30 years that some Black Boys, who are raised by single Black Moms, get into trouble because of their inability to logically think through a problem utilizing choices and consequences. Instead, their conclusions are driven by their emotions. Many times, this behavior is taught by their mother. This behavior that the mom is teaching is called "outer-directed negative emotions." Many of these moms are not aware that they are using outer-directed negative behavior. They often use outer-directed negative emotions when disciplining or punishing the boy. This irrational negative behavior can come in the form of rage, hatred, or disrespect. This frequently occurs when they can't already handle or manage their actions and feelings toward the father or some other man who has mistreated them. Without intentionally doing so, they are teaching their sons to react irrationally when they become fearful, enraged, angry, or upset. I am not saying that these women are morally inferior to men because they base moral judgments by using outer-directed negative emotions rather than logic to make some decisions. However, when Black Boys are affected by negative emotions, unsympathetic feelings, and negative perceptions it will play a major role in most of their decision-making process.

Again, remember these outer-directed negative emotions are usually applied when the mother is disciplining or punishing the boy. For example, if the father does not send the alimony for the month, she becomes very angered and disgusted with the boy's father, resulting in an improper reaction toward the boy by hitting or spanking when it is not called for. Therefore, many Black Teens and Young Adults solve their problems with others by resulting by using violence. These teens would say, "He took advantage of me I am going to get him back." Adding the factor that so many Black Boys have a fascination with guns, they end up killing someone.

Recent experimental studies from the National Library of Medicine and the National Center for Biotechnological Information show that emotions can significantly affect how we think, decide, and solve problems. Women mix reasoning and emotion together to problem solve – men tend to focus primarily on reasoning to problem solve. This is why men tend to zero in on one issue solely to resolve problems. Women engage multiple intelligences together to resolve issues (Weber, 2009). Logic is the study of the principles of deductive reasoning and can be considered a valid system or mode of reasoning. A child learns how to problem-solve by observing the examples placed before him or her. Many problems will occur in a boy's life if he is taught to use multiple intelligences to include emotions rather than logic alone when making life decisions (Weber, 2009). Boys who grow up in single-parent homes, with the mother as the lead, often do not learn how to control their emotions. This leads to them not being able to cope with conflict in life.

A boy must grow up to learn discipline and self-control to navigate life in the real world. When he is raised to think logically by his father or other positive men, he learns the self-control that allows him to walk away from trouble. He thinks about the long-term effects of choices, the consequences of his actions, and the impact on others. Though many times, when he is raised by a woman, he learns to act on his feelings rather than thinking logically. This behavior can cause him to often say and do things he regrets later.

A man who has no control over his emotions is more prone to go into fits of rage, getting arrested for domestic violence, or getting into fights over silly things like a basketball game. His words and actions can cause him to get into a scuffle with police, where he can be fatally shot and killed for resisting arrest. This loss of self-control can cause him to be seen as weak by his peers and make him a target for others who think like him. Therefore, many Black Boys go to prison for gun violence based on shooting someone who made them angry over a girl, gangs, drugs, or money.

OVERPROTECTING YOUR SONS

The term "helicopter parent" is used a lot with adolescents or even adult children, it and refers to trying to always be involved in every aspect of that child's life, not just in a supportive way, but in a controlling way. So often, this can be difficult for the child and end up causing stress or tension because of an overprotective mother. Studies have shown that boys of overprotective moms have difficulty making decisions and lack the ability to become a success as an adult. A Black Boy whose mom is overprotective does not know how to deal with adversities and the ups and downs of life. Most of these boys have a lack of patience for problem-solving and when they are confronted with having to be decisive in making life decisions, they do not do well.

Many overprotective moms believe their child is never lying. This can cause bad behavior in the child. When the boy does something wrong, many overprotective moms make excuses for them. When they make mistakes, they blame others for their child's actions. And when they mess up in life, they are always there to bail them out. If children are not held accountable for their actions, they will grow up to be irresponsible adults who blame everyone else for their circumstances.

CHAPTER 5

"THE TALK"

"THE TALK" HAS BECOME ESSENTIAL FOR DECADES AS THEY DEAL WITH THE RACIAL DIVIDE

THE TALK: A GENERATIONAL PRACTICE

For generations, "The Talk" has been a conversation conducted in African American families. "The Talk" is an informal discussion Black parents have with their children, especially teenagers, about the dangers they face due to racism or the unjust treatment from authority figures, law enforcement or other parties, and how to de-escalate them. Variations of "The Talk" have been conducted in Black families for decades; the practice dates back to slavery and has lasted centuries. At some point, Black children all get warnings from elders about how to avoid and survive encounters with the police or incidents due to racism. The premature deaths, as far back as Emmett Till, age 14, up to the death of Trayvon Martin, age 17, occurred because they were viewed through a distorted lens. American culture often defines Black males negatively and far too narrowly. In simple terms, there is much more to young men of color beyond the stereotypical images portrayed in our society.

"The Talk" is a practice that occurs in Black homes whether they live in the eastern, western, northern, or southern parts of this country. This conversation happens no matter the socioeconomic status or profession. It even occurs in families where a parent is a member of law enforcement. This dialogue is very uncomfortable, but for many Black households, "The Talk" has become essential for decades as they deal with the racial divide.

HOW MAINSTREAM AMERICA VIEWS BLACK BOYS AS A THREAT

As many Black Boys grow up, they often do not know that mainstream America views them as a threat; in fact, the larger they are in stature, the more frightened people tend to be. Neil Hester and Kurt Gray from the Department of Psychology and Neuroscience at the University of North Carolina at Chapel Hill stated young Black men are stereotyped as threatening (Hester & Gray, 2018). This can have grave consequences for interactions with police. Hester and Gray's research indicates that these threatening stereotypes are even greater for tall Black men, who face greater discrimination from police officers and provoke adverse responses (Hester & Gray, 2018). We challenge the assumption that height is intrinsically good for men. White men may benefit from height, but Black men may not. More broadly, we demonstrate how demographic factors (e.g., race) can influence how people interpret physical traits (e.g., height and size). This difference in interpretation is a matter not of magnitude but of meaning; the same trait is positive for some groups of people but negative for others.

When Black Boys react emotionally, mainstream America normally interprets this behavior as threatening. What I have been able to observe is that when these emotional reactions occur, white officers tend to respond in a violent manner instead of finding other means of de-escalating the situation. Social Workers and educators who see young people — especially Black boys who live in poor, segregated neighborhoods — reacting aggressively, becoming irritable, or having trouble concentrating, often identify such behavior as maladaptive. But new research, led by Noni Gaylord-Harden, a clinical psychologist at Texas A&M University, proposes that young people's behavior is a rational response to their environment and helps keep them safe. Her findings suggest that instead of focusing on these behaviors by identifying them as disorders to be punished or symptoms to be treated, policymakers need to recognize them as adaptive and work to change the inequitable environment that produces them (Harris, 2021).

The stereotyping of Black boys as young as 10 may have caused them to not be viewed in the same light of childhood innocence as their white peers. They are instead more likely to be mistaken as older, be perceived as guilty, and face police violence if accused of a crime, according to research published by the American Psychological Association (Goff, 2014). Stereotypes have a long and complicated history in the USA, widely influencing African-American males who are the most visibly stereotyped racial group in the USA (Harpalnai 2017). Because of this stereotyping of Black males, many Black parents have had to have "The Talk." As stated previously, the practice dates back generations and is often a rite of passage for Black children.

HOW "THE TALK" LEAD TO BOOKS, DOCUMENTARIES, AND TELEVISION SHOWS

The acknowledgment of this topic has led to "The Talk" being the conversation of many books, documentaries, and television shows. The New York Times made a short documentary in 2015 featuring the experiences of Black Americans in having this conversation with their children and their memories of their own parents' conversations with them. A 2016 episode of Black-ish featured three generations of a Black family watching television as a verdict in a police brutality case was announced; ABC rebroadcast it June 2, 2020, in response to the George Floyd killing and protests. PBS created a two-hour documentary, The Talk: Race in America, in 2017. Procter & Gamble produced a commercial called "The Talk" in 2017. A 2018 episode of Grey's Anatomy included a Black couple having the talk with their son. A 2018 book for 4-to-8-year-olds, Something Happened in Our Town, recommends having the first talk prior to preschool and another when they start venturing independently into public space.

WHEN SHOULD BLACK BOYS RECEIVE THE TALK?

Many members of the majority community get these negative stereotypes in the media and apply these ideas, often subconsciously. This subconscious behavior will have them feeling threatened by young Black males walking behind them or sitting across the room from them. This behavior can even flow into the classroom where both classmates and teachers of these young Black boys feel threatened. They often see them as inherently bad and malicious soon-to-be criminals. To make matters worse, the recent killings of Eric Garner, Michael Brown, and George Floyd, among others, serve as grim reminders to young, disadvantaged men of color that their lives are undervalued in their own country. The cumulative impact of these tragedies on youth is what some scholars call a "speaking wound," when such events echo similar treatment others have faced (Dutro & Bien, 2014).

"It is easier to build strong children than to repair broken men." - Frederick Douglass. These killings re-trigger in young men traumatic memories of racially charged encounters with strangers and police encounters that could have easily ended much worse. As shared by Gustavo Solis in the USC News and Trojan Family Magazine, different versions of "The Talk" have been around for generations, each one with a specific set of warnings about the times.

For example, Najuma Smith-Pollard remembers her grandfather telling stories about being taught to avoid certain sidewalks and neighborhoods while growing up in Mississippi in the 1940s. Now the program manager for the USC Cecil Murray Center for Community Engagement, Smith-Pollard thinks back to her time as an associate minister with the First African Methodist Episcopal Church in Los Angeles. Groups of male volunteers used to talk to young Black boys about how to dress, walk, act, and to be mindful of how others could perceive them. This was before the city's 1992 riots. With today's prevalence of video technology and the heightened focus on shootings of unarmed Black men, the current version of "The Talk" now focuses more on interacting with law enforcement than avoiding certain neighborhoods, she said. But regardless of which specific threat is prioritized, she added, the substance of "The Talk" and the reason behind it remains the same: "It is a conversation about safety because we have a profiling problem" (Solis, 2021).

I started receiving The Talk when I was around eight or nine years old. I received this conversation from my parents, aunts and uncles, and even friends' parents while growing up. They all told me to be respectful and keep my temper no matter what. My mom got real specific when I was twelve years old. She talked about what to do when confronted by the police; she said to keep my hands visible at all times. Don't make any sudden movements. Say, "Yes, sir," and "No, sir." Don't give them a reason to use force on you. She also told me you are a big boy, so do not speak loud or aggressively to any authority figure. She said believe it or not, your size can frighten them. You are not to express your anger, disgust, fear, anxiety, or sadness by what you say or any type of non-verbal communication. I was to do just what the officer told me to do, even if I knew I had not done anything wrong. She said you are doing this because you do not want to be seen as a threat to the police officer, as well as, I want you to come home alive.

"The Talk" must be given by single Black mothers. It must become a rite of passage for Black moms' and their sons'. They must start teaching them before they go out into the world on their own and continue as they get older. They must be taught how they are to act when confronted by the police and other authority figures. Explain to them this is being done to reduce the possibility of any type of conflict with police officers, teachers, principals, or any other person in charge of them. Mothers cannot wait for someone else to have this discussion with their child. These moms must understand that, at some point, their son will go from being seen as an innocent young man to being considered a threat. These single Black moms must have these difficult conversations with their sons as police shootings of Black men under questionable circumstances continue to occur across cities in the United States.

THE DOS AND DON'TS WHEN BLACK BOYS DEAL WITH THE POLICE

TO HELP THOSE MOMS WITH THAT CONVERSATION, HERE ARE SOME DOS AND DON'TS WHEN YOUR BLACK BOYS ARE STOPPED BY THE POLICE

The following guides were compiled with information sourced from the American Civil Liberties Union (ACLU).

THE DOS WHEN YOU ARE STOPPED AS A PEDESTRIAN

- **DO** know that the police may stop and question you for any reason at all. You don't have to look suspicious or be a potential witness to a crime.
- Unless police have a reasonable suspicion, based on specific and clearly describable facts, along with reasonable assumptions, for suspecting that you committed, are committing, or are about to commit a crime, you are generally free to leave.
- During a stop, the police can ask about your name, address, and age. In California, you cannot be arrested for refusing to provide your I.D.
- **DO** ask, "am I free to leave?" If they say yes, calmly leave.
- **DO** exercise your right to remain silent. Say, "**I want to remain silent.**" You legally cannot be arrested or detained for refusing to answer questions. However, it could look suspicious to the police if you answer questions and then suddenly stop, which could lead to an illegal arrest. Make it your practice to always remain silent.

IF YOU ARE STOPPED FOR QUESTIONING, DON'T...

- **DON'T** try to run away. Many Black and Brown people have been shot in the back while running away from the police.
- **DON'T** physically resist a "pat-down" or search because this could lead to an officer illegally using force against you. Say, "**I do not consent to a search.**"
- **DON'T** disrespect a police officer. Although you have a constitutional right to do so, it could lead to your arrest or physical harm.
- **DON'T** lie. Say, "**I want to remain silent.**"
- **DON'T** forget that police are legally allowed to lie, intimidate, and bluff you.
- Only discuss your citizenship/immigration status with your lawyer.

IF YOU ARE SEARCHED...

- **DO** remember they must have at least some reasonable suspicion that you have been involved in a crime or are armed.
- **DO** ensure the officer knows you do not agree to being searched (they might search you anyway, but calmly and safely make your opposition known). Say, "**I do not consent to a search.**"
- Be aware a police officer may pat down your outer clothing only. Police cannot squeeze or reach into your pockets unless they believe they have felt a weapon or contraband (like a baggie of unlawful drugs) after patting you down. If the police develop probable cause for

believing that you have committed a crime, they can broaden their search.
- **DO** give your name and birth date if you are being given a ticket and sign the ticket. If you don't, you may be arrested.

IF YOU ARE SEARCHED...

- **DON'T** empty your pockets or reach towards your waistband as the officer approaches. Many Black and Brown people have been shot by police officers who falsely claimed they were reaching for a gun in their waistband.

THE DO'S AND DON'TS OF POLICE CAR STOPS

If you are pulled over in a traffic stop and have a hands-free phone station in your vehicle, consider turning on your camera to record the interaction. Make sure to do this before the officer gets out of the police car so they don't see you and mistakenly think you are reaching for a weapon.

IF YOU ARE STOPPED IN YOUR CAR, DO...

- **DO** remember that the police must have a reasonable suspicion for believing that you have committed a traffic violation or criminal offense.
- **DO** keep your hands on the wheel and let the officer know what you are doing for your safety. Say, "I'm going

to reach for my registration now." Many Black and Brown people have been shot and killed when police claimed they made sudden hand movements.
- **DO** show your license, registration, and proof of insurance when asked.
- **DO** sign your ticket if you are given one. Otherwise, you may be arrested.
- **DO** take the DUI test if you are arrested unless you are willing to risk your license being suspended. Before you are arrested, you may refuse to take the Preliminary Alcohol Screening (PAS) breathalyzer test unless you are under the age of 21.
- **DO** keep your car interior clear of unnecessary objects. It may give the police a reason to search the car. If they see anything illegal, this may create probable cause for them to search you or your car. They cannot search the trunk unless they have your consent, a search warrant, or probable cause to believe the trunk contains evidence of a crime.
- **DO** say, "**I do not consent to a search.**"

IF YOU ARE STOPPED IN YOUR CAR, DON'T...

- **DON'T** physically resist a search. Say, "**I do not consent to a search.**"
- **DON'T** refuse to sign a ticket. You can be arrested for it.
- **DON'T** search for your license or registration until you are asked to provide it. Let the officer know what you are doing for your safety. Say, "I'm going to reach for

my registration now." Many Black and Brown people have been shot and killed when police claimed they made sudden hand movements.
- **DON'T** disrespect the officer. Although you have a constitutional right to do so, it could lead to your arrest.
- **DON'T** attempt to bribe the police.

THE DO'S AND DON'TS OF ARRESTS

IF YOU ARE ARRESTED OR TAKEN TO A POLICE STATION, DO...

- **DO** ask if you can park your car in a safe place or have a licensed driver take it away if you are arrested. This will avoid expensive towing or impoundment fees.
- If the police arrest you, they must have probable cause for believing that you have committed a crime.
- **DO** tell the police your name and basic identifying information. But nothing else.
- **DO** say, "**I want to remain silent**" and clearly state, "**I want to talk to a lawyer.**" They should stop questioning you after that. If they do not stop questioning, calmly and clearly repeat that you want to remain silent and that you want to speak to a lawyer.
- **DO** make sure you get your three phone calls within three hours of getting arrested or immediately after being booked. You can call a lawyer, bail bondsman, relative, or any other person. If you have children under

18, you get two additional calls to arrange childcare. Memorize important phone numbers.
- **DO** assume the police are recording your calls (except calls to your lawyer).

IF YOU ARE ARRESTED OR TAKEN TO A POLICE STATION, DON'T...

- **DON'T** try to run, resist, fight back, or reach suddenly for any items in your pockets or clothing, as this could lead to law enforcement causing you physical harm.
- **DON'T** give them any information except for your name and basic identifying information.
- **DON'T** give explanations, excuses, or stories. Say, "**I want to remain silent**," and, "**I want to talk to a lawyer.**"
- **DON'T** consent to any searches or give up your right to a lawyer.
- **DON'T** talk about your case on the phone. The police might be recording your phone calls (except those to your lawyer).
- **DON'T** make any decisions in your case without talking to a lawyer first.
- **DON'T** discuss your citizenship or immigration status with anyone other than your lawyer.

THE POLICE ARE AT MY DOOR

YOUR RIGHTS AND HOW TO REDUCE RISK TO YOURSELF

- You should not invite the officer into your house. Talk with the officers through the door and ask them to show you identification. You do not have to let them in unless they can show you a warrant signed by a judicial officer that lists your address as a place to be searched or that has your name on it as the subject of an arrest warrant.
- Ask the officer to slip the warrant under the door or hold it up to the window so you can read it. A search warrant allows police to enter the address listed on the warrant, but officers can only search the areas and for the items listed. An arrest warrant has the name of the person to be arrested.
- Even if officers have a warrant, you have the right to remain silent. You should not answer questions or speak to the officers while they are in your house conducting their search. Stand silently and observe what they do, where they go, and what they take. Write down everything you observed as soon as you can.

<u>WHEN YOUR RIGHTS HAVE BEEN VIOLATED</u>

- Write down everything you remember, including officers' badge and patrol car numbers, which agency the officers were from, and any other details. Get contact information for witnesses.
- File a written complaint with the agency's internal affairs division or civilian complaint board. In most

cases, you can file a complaint anonymously if you wish.

HOW TO BE A RESPONSIBLE BYSTANDER

- If you are a guest inside the house and end up answering the door, you should make clear to the police that you are a guest and do not have the authority to let them inside without the homeowner's permission.

DR. CALVIN AVANT

CHAPTER 6

BLACK BOYS IN A SELF CRISIS

SELF-IMAGE | SELF-ESTEEM

SELF-DISCIPLINE | SELF-RESPECT

SELF-REALIZATION

BLACK BOYS IN A SELF CRISIS

Black Boys are at high risk of a non-productive lifestyle and failing academically, socially, emotionally, and economically in life. This non-productive lifestyle starts at birth and persists on into adulthood. Frequently, this non-productive lifestyle is a result of being born in poverty, in a single-parent-family home headed by a female with no dad (no role model), or to a dead-beat dad (negative role model). This crisis is a direct correlation to my belief that the absence of Black male teachers in school and fathers at home has had a negative impact on Black Boys.

Countless Black Boys grow up in poverty in a segregated community where they are not exposed to the protective factors that could lead them towards those positive patterns needed to become self-assured, successful Black Men. Protective factors are present in activities such as pee-wee football, martial arts, soccer, dance, etc. These activities often provide positive, encouraging role models that impart discipline. Segregated and impoverished communities lack the resources to participate in these activities that provide the aforementioned protective factors.

Because of the following prolonged traumatic events while struggling toward manhood, many Black Boys have a poor self-image, lack self-esteem, and lack self-respect, creating a destructive lifestyle:

1. Lack of exposure to successful Black Male models in their daily lives
2. Lack of exposure to a world outside of the community they live in
3. Inability to see their self-worth
4. Making decisions using only emotions rather than integrating logic into the decision-making process
5. Poor social skills
6. Many health deficiencies
7. Inability to set and achieve goals
8. Lacking academic success that cause them to drop out of school

Prolonged lack of exposure to many of these protective factors can cause Black Boys to not mature and grow up having the same norms as society. They do not recognize that their actions are unacceptable to society causing many of them to live non-productive lives. Many of the risk factors causing a non-productive lifestyle were modeled by their parents, peers, and residents in the communities they grew up in. The risk factors they were taught are recognized as acceptable conduct in these communities. These unacceptable behaviors have caused many Black Boys to not gain the capacity to transition successfully into adulthood and achieve economic self-sufficiency. Without outside intervention from sources who understand their inability to recognize their reliance on these destructive behaviors, they will never learn how to accept society norms and become productive citizens.

Their parents are also susceptible to the same characteristics in their lives. Many of the characteristics that have been formed were created over several generations. These patterns have been passed on for at least the last three generations in the Black community. Many families have become reliant on these negative patterns, which have caused them to become dependent on dysfunctional lifestyles such as:

1. Living on public assistance and in public housing for a lifetime
2. Have more children to increase their public assistance provisions
3. Lack of Commitment in Relationships
    a. Shacking/never getting married
    b. Divorce
    c. Promiscuity
    d. Having children out of wedlock
    e. Having children with multiple partners
4. Prison recidivism

    a. Criminal behavior
    b. Hustling
    c. Buying stolen goods
5. Never owning property
6. Substance abusers and alcoholics
7. Deadbeat dads
8. Not seeing the importance of education

STEPS TO ADDRESSING THE SELF CRISIS

Black Boys are faced with many challenges in today's society. These challenges range from racism, academic underachievement, family problems, as well as a lack of positive role models. But one of the most overlooked challenges facing Black Boys is their lack of a positive self-image. This poor self-image in Black Boys includes them dealing with their own self-hate, self-doubt, shame, guilt, and anger. Self-image is the result of life experiences and is a product of an individual's early relationships, particularly with their father.

The Black Family is where Black Boys should learn the values, morals, and ethics that will carry them through life. This is where the parents should be there for support and encouragement of their positive self-worth. The boy needs to be aware that parents are their first role models, not some rap star. Black Boys act out what they see parents, peers, and community members do. Dr. Jawanza Kunjufu stated in his groundbreaking book, Developing Positive Self-Images and Discipline for Black Children, that all teachers, parents, and especially adult Black males have failed to provide the support and discipline needed to keep Black Boys off the streets and in the classroom. Black males are caught in a self-perpetuating cycle of failure. The absence of stable, successful Black male role models ensures that young Black Boys will do poorly in school, turn to street life, and father yet another generation of boys who do not value their self-worth.

Black Boys need a sense of belonging, and this is something that a strong family structure and the black church family can provide. Black Boys need to be loved and affirmed as being the beautiful people that they are, says Enoch H. Oglesby. A Black Boy must know who he is and how to self-discipline himself. Black Boys need positive mentorship by successful and concerned Black men, in addition to exposure to alternative positive concepts, strategies, and opportunities, which will cause them to make choices that will enable them to thrive as individuals and as leaders in the community.

We must teach Black Boys that skin color is not a predictor of self-efficacy (self-worth). First and foremost, we must teach dark skin Black Boys to not negatively self-evaluate themselves. They learn negative self-evaluation from the media and often white America, who will give the impression that dark skin Black young men are dangerous and are predisposed to criminal behavior. You must find challenging tasks and help these boys succeed. Dark skin Black Boys who experience success in their everyday life will feel more confident and empowered to have control and manage their lives.

DEVELOPING A POSITIVE SELF-IMAGE

RECOGNIZING HOW I SEE MYSELF

You must help the boy recognize when he has negatively self-evaluated himself. Signs of this internal battle are apprehension, feeling helpless, being disillusioned, or dejected, blaming oneself, and having no incentive to succeed. Once the boy recognizes when he is negatively self-evaluating, he can identify those signs causing him to not think positively about himself and the ability to successfully accomplish the task at hand. When the young man negatively self-evaluates himself, it can cause him to make poor decisions. He must learn how to detect when he is negatively self-evaluating. First, he must recognize his internal feelings, both physically and emotionally. It might be helpful to have him keep a journal on those internal feelings. They can be short statements such as:

- "I stress out when taking a test"
- "Sometimes I wake up mad"
- "I'm dumb"
- "No one likes me"

He should write down what he detects when this negative self-evaluation is occurring. Remember, if you do not see something as being a problem, you will never seek a solution for it.

DEVELOP SELF-TALK

We must help the boy to develop the skill of self-talk. Self-talk is your internal dialogue. It's influenced by your subconscious mind, and it reveals your thoughts, beliefs, questions, and ideas. Self-talk can be both negative and positive. It can help you be a more positive person, and it may improve your health and decision making. Developing self-talk does not happen overnight; it takes lots of practice. We are to teach our boys how to focus their self-talk on not just surviving but thriving and moving forward in life, which can provide essential motivation to achieve goals. They must be taught how to begin identifying their strengths. Yet, it is much easier for us to identify our weaknesses than our strengths. You can help the boy nurture his strengths by brainstorming on strengths and helping him to use his strengths more often. Making a list of all his strengths and posting it on the wall, in his notebook or on the refrigerator, where he can see them daily is important. Continuously discuss both self-talk and his strengths. Being repetitive can help make the information stick. Teaching the boy to use self-talk will aid him seeing a wider view of his life and opportunities, rather than just narrowly focusing on threats. When teaching the concept of self-talk, instruct the boys how to acknowledge and directly address their doubts and fears; this can help promote happiness, well-being, and success in their lives.

GETTING RID OF THE NEGATIVE VOICES IN THEIR HEAD

Many Black Boys I have spoken to have said there is a voice inside my head that keeps saying to me that – "I am a loser; I will mess up things for sure." These negative voices have a sense of emotional urgency that demands our attention. Many of these negative voices are fear-based, self-protective factors usually used during their worst times when they are in dire need of help. These situations most likely happen during their pre-teen phase when they start experiencing life. Unlike adults they can't make a choice to not listen to their negative voices. It sometimes becomes difficult for these boys to ignore or avoid them, resulting in unhealthy social and academic decisions. So, as parents, we must address the issue. You must start by teaching the boy that no matter what the negative voice in his head is saying, he is to never quit no matter what. Teach him to never assume he can't accomplish a task. He must learn that there is an answer to every problem, so he can't give up.

A lack of self-assurance is often the cause of these boys continuously negatively self-evaluating themselves. If the boy is always belittling himself saying things like:

- I'm dumb
- I'm ugly
- I can't make the team
- I can't get that job

These statements become self-fulfilling prophecies. They are becoming what they have self-evaluated. The next time they start negatively self-evaluating themselves get them to flip the switch and start stating positive affirmation such as:

- I am worthy
- I am loved
- I love myself
- No one can stop me from fulfilling my purpose
- I am committed to doing great things
- I come from a rich Black heritage

Get them to keep it up until the thoughts have transitioned to thinking they can succeed. Tell and show them that you love them. Help them find inspiration and the desire to succeed. Finally, help them find someone to talk to, preferably a Black male mentor or counselor; an adult besides the parent to help give direction.

BLACK BOYS WITH POOR SELF-ESTEEM

Self-image is how we imagine ourselves to be, and self-esteem is how we feel about that image, says Drs. Darlene Hopson and Derek S. Hopson. The Hopsons stated that self-esteem can be taught. Creating high self-esteem is a critical concept that we must help Black Boys develop. With high self-esteem, many Black Boys will have the courage to take the risk of doing things others around them have not tried. By taking these risks, they will develop new skills and abilities to become acquainted with people outside of their world. This will help them stop negative self-evaluation and stay on a path of success. When a boy has low self-esteem, he is less likely to step out and try new things, acquire new skills, and get to know people outside of his environment.

Also, low self-esteem can cause him to be influenced by peer pressure and negative people in the street. This behavior can easily cause negative self-evaluation that could be translated into failing in life. During their growth and development, a boys' self-esteem is affected in three areas: Family, School and Community.

FAMILY

The family is widely seen as an important influence on self-esteem because it is where the initial sense of oneself is formed. The effects of low self-esteem on the family can be reflected outwardly toward siblings and parents through verbal or physical expression. Many boys with self-esteem difficulties have absorbed negative things said about them by parents, peers, and others, such as:

- "You are going to be just like your no-good daddy!"
- "You are a cry-baby!"
- "You are a sissy!"
- "You are stupid, fat or lazy!"

As they begin to define themselves in light of their low sense of self, they may undertake the views that they are the negative things others are saying about them. Some things parents can do to help raise a Black Boys Self- Esteem:

MONITOR THE MUSIC THEY LISTEN TO

a. Listening to rap stars use terms such as nigga, bitch, or thug and other negative statements can create those negative voices in their head, pointing them toward a destructive lifestyle. They can start portraying what they hear in this music. These rappers become their role models, and they start believing this is who they are and start emulating what they hear and believe.

MONITOR THE TELEVISION THEY WATCH

a. Studies from Medical Daily have shown that television can decrease self-esteem in Black Boys and Girls.

b. Regarding Black Boys, television tends to often criminalize them in many programs, show them as hoodlums and buffoons, and without many varieties in the kinds of roles they occupy.

PARENTS AS MODELS

a. The old saying of, "the parent is the child's first teacher" could not be more true. You are their first experience as they enter the world. You are who feeds their soul, intellect, humanity, and capacity. Your role is far more vital than the school teacher. Teachers can care for your child at school and give them knowledge and experience in a controlled environment; however, it is you who aids them through life. There is a "prepared environment" for school, so you should prepare the environment of home for success by employing the following:

1. Providing a stable home environment
2. Sitting down together for meals
3. Read to and with your son
4. Help to develop early social skills that match society's norms
5. Help establish family values and morals
6. Help develop emotional awareness and how they should react to them
7. Model positive behavior, not a "Do as I say and not as I do" attitude.

<u>SCHOOL</u>

a. In American classrooms—including preschool classrooms—studies show that Black Boys are more likely to be seen as "problem" children than their peers, and they are less likely to be considered ready for school (Wright, 2019). These boys appear to be hesitant and uncomfortable in the classroom. They tend to only answer direct questions and prefer to keep their opinions to themselves because they fear the reactions of others. Guarded behaviors and minimal interactions with other classmates lessen their social impact on others, which reinforces their belief of having nothing to offer others.

b. As parents, you need to enroll your boy in schools that have culturally responsive teachers who will help affirm

Black Boys by incorporating books, visuals, and other materials that reflect Black histories, lives, and points of view. This kind of exposure is critical to the boys' development of a healthy sense of self. Learning about the important discoveries and courageous acts of Black boys and men from the past and present can serve as an important reminder for today's Black Boys to see themselves and their communities as vital parts of American history (Wright, 2019). It also empowers them to challenge the "troublemaker" and "bad boy" stereotypes found in typical portrayals of Black Boys (Wright, 2019).

c. Black male students benefit from having a Black male teacher. "Kids do better when they're taught by teachers who look like them. "That's just the way it is," states California State University, Northridge (CSUN) education professor David Kretschmer. "That's why we need more men of color in American classrooms, period." Kretschmer codirects the Future Minority Male Teachers Across California Project (F2MTC), which seeks to recruit, prepare, and retain male teachers of color at the elementary level in California's university system (Hobbs, 2020). After the 1954 Brown v. Board of Education Supreme Court ruling, African American teachers were pushed out of schools and out of the teaching profession to make integration more appealing to white families (Pollard, 2020.) Many white families did not want their children to be taught by African American teachers (Pollard, 2020). As stated in The Hidden Cost of Brown v. Board, Black students lost role models who not only knew them on a personal level, but had a unique understanding of their communities, cultural identities, and individual situations. Many blacks believed that "without the principals, the members of the African American community lost their voice in education, and the students also lost role models whom they were able to trust and emulate." Because education was one of the most well-respected career paths open to blacks, there was an abundance of well-trained, talented black teachers.

d. Black Boys who have Black male teachers have high self-esteem, lower dropout rates, fewer disciplinary issues, more positive views of schooling, and better test scores. Decades of research link African American youths' high self-esteem and positive racial identity with their academic success, behavioral adjustment, and positive emotional functioning (Chavous, Rivas-Drake, Smalls, Griffin, & Cogburn, 2008; Prinz, 2009; Smith, Levine, Smith, E. P., Dumas, J., & Prinz, R. J. (2009). Given the race-related disparities for health and well-being found in children of color in the United States, it is particularly critical to understand the protective function of self-esteem and positive racial identity among these youths. Recent data highlights disparities in health and well-being experienced by children based on their race/ethnicity (Okeke-Adeyanju et al., 2014) (Hernandez & Napierala, 2013). If you have Black male teachers in your son's school at his grade level, request that your child be placed in his classroom. I remember when I was teaching third grade in a title-one elementary school in Florida, a fellow teacher brought her son to me and requested that he be placed in my class. She said that she saw this as an opportunity for her son to have another positive Black male role model in his life besides his dad. Having at least one Black teacher in elementary school cuts the high school dropout rates of very low-income Black boys by 39% and raises college aspirations among poor students of both sexes by 19%, according to a 2017 study by researchers from Johns Hopkins University, American University and the University of California, Davis (Gershenson et al., 2017). Also, advocate for your school to invite black males from the community to serve as role models and support. If those things are not in your school, it is your responsibility to ensure that your son gets positive role models in his life. Seek out your community, churches, and family members to help so these boys can be involved with positive Black men in order to see what a confident, successful Black man looks like. This was stated in an article written by Dr. William Hobbs of Florida Memorial University, which is an HBCU, "I Become What I See": Addressing Academic Patterning Distress and the Importance of Black Male Teachers (Hobbs, 2020).

e. My sister Norma Jean was a single Black mom who would always complain that she did not have enough money to pay her bills. Yet she would find the funds to pay for her son's participation in football, basketball, baseball, bowling, and other male-dominated activities. She put her son around positive Black men. It is my belief that a boy learns to be a positive man by being around positive men. She went even further; by the time he was 12 years old, she started sending him each summer to stay with me and my family. He came every summer until he was 19 years old. The time spent with me allowed him to see how a nuclear family (husband & wife and their children) lives and especially see me in my role as a father. He is now married with three kids and is a certified aircraft mechanic. Dr. Jawanza Kujufu, a noted author and Chicago educator, says that raising a boy is very hard on a single mother. It's more challenging when there is no male role model in the home for the boy to emulate. Consequently, the mother will have to introduce her son to Black male role models in their extended family, such as grandfathers, uncles, cousins, and nephews, along with church members, friends, coaches, and co-workers. In an effort to address this initiative, President Obama established My Brother's Keeper, which evolved into My Brother's Keeper Alliance (MBK Alliance) and is focused on "building safe and supportive communities for boys and young men of color where they feel valued and have clear pathways to opportunity" (Fink, 2018). The organization provides financial and logistical support to evidence-based programs that make a positive difference in boys' lives and has been instrumental in connecting boys with adult male mentors (Fink, 2018).

COMMUNITY

a. Boys with low self-esteem hesitate when interacting with groups of neighborhood kids or joining social activities, such as parties or games. They generally wait to be invited to play or join others, but then only participate minimally when they agree to play. Their guardedness and self-doubt hold them back from fully interacting with others, again reinforcing their negative self-image.

b. The following are five building blocks of self-esteem that many Black Boys do not have or are not taught that would help enhance their self-esteem:

1. A safe environment - both physically and psychologically
2. Identity - knowing "who I am"
3. Belonging - knowing "who I am a part of"
4. Competence – feeling or believing that you can do something well or succeed at something
5. Have purpose and set goals that contribute to the needs of self and the group

As parents, you need to start thinking about how to ensure that these concepts are in place from infancy to help build self-esteem on several levels, such as: developmental, racial, and cultural. Black Boys must learn not only basic developmental tasks, but also:

a. What it means to be a member of a minority group/African American
b. "The Talk" — a discussion left almost exclusively to Black parents and family members about police, even when the parent is a police officer. "The Talk" will be discussed at length in Chapter 5.

DEVELOP POSITIVE SELF-ESTEEM IN BLACK BOYS

Let's look at basic developmental issues and see how we can provide the opportunity for Black Boys to build high self-esteem.

SAFETY

a. As a parent, you need to provide the boy with a safe environment to live in where he can explore his surroundings. This safe environment must be both physical and psychological. The psychological safety includes safeguarding the boy from persons who talk negatively about their self-worth. Black Boys who have chronic low self-esteem tend to agree with others' negative evaluations and opinions of themselves. However, they would prefer to think of themselves in a more positive manner. They tend to value themselves to the extent they have felt valued. They lose interest in mastering skills and tasks and continuously compare themselves to others, which results in feelings of worthlessness and the expectation of failing at most attempted tasks. One thing you, as the parent, can do to combat this behavior is use plenty of praise. Give praise, recognition, a special privilege, or increased responsibility for a job well done. Emphasize the good things that they do, not just what they do wrong. Intentionally, catch the child in the act of being good.

IDENTITY AND BELONGING - IDENTITY DEVELOPMENT IS A JOURNEY AND NOT A DESTINATION

a. They need to learn what is expected of members of these groups, and how these groups are evaluated by others. For example, children are learning what behaviors are "expected" of boys or girls as youth go on into adulthood. Black men, fathers, and mentors must learn to get in touch with their own process of healing so that they can be role models to these boys. Black men sometimes face the inability to express their fears and emotions about getting a job, dealing with discrimination, and also with overcoming perceived inadequacies. Once these men understand where they are in their struggle, then they can pass that knowledge on to their sons or mentees.

1. It is important for Black Boys to define themselves for themselves.
2. It is important that we affirm the identities of Black Boys.

3. It is important for Black Boys to have resources to help them constructively.
4. It is important for Black Boys to evaluate the images and portrayals they see of themselves in society.
5. It is important that Black Boys give a name and meaning to their experiences.
6. It is important that Black Boys are able to identify inequities and racism.
7. Black Boys need to know that it is okay to feel vulnerable.

EMBRACING RACIAL-ETHNIC IDENTITY

a. Feeling good about and connected to your ethnic group is positively associated with school performance, mental well-being, and good physical health. Black Boys might not always experience welcoming or affirming spaces in school. They may face stereotypes about their academic abilities, not see people like them represented in school materials, or experience disproportionately harsh discipline. Feeling a sense of pride in and a strong connection to one's ethnic background gives Black Boys a source from which to draw strength. This can be an important asset in the face of adversity.

b. Talk about different shades of skin, hairstyles, and other forms of "variation" among humans with the goal to "normalize" human differences. Also, as they get older talk, about biases and stereotypes in everyday life. When boys are in elementary school, parents can get into the "deeper meanings" of structural inequalities, like why people of color are not represented in social studies textbooks as much as white people (Mader, 2019).

c. When children as young as 4 or 5 years old watch television and parents notice stereotypes or the absence of diversity, parents should mention that. It could be as simple as pointing out, "There are no kids that look racially different on this show being friends" (Mader, 2019).

<u>LEARNING FAMILY VALUES</u>

a. Do not assume your child knows or understands your family values. It is the parent's responsibility to communicate their family morals and values to their son. Also, you must tell your son, as a member of your family, that he is expected to abide by those values. When communicating these family morals and values, you must be very specific and clear. Let your son know that you are not just being nosy but have their best interest at heart. Express that it is your responsibility to observe and correct any negative behavior that could cause him to become involved in behaviors that can be detrimental to him. Explain to your son your family's guideline for borrowing things from others. Explain that use and abuse of drugs and alcohol will not be tolerated because he is harming his body and dishonoring the family's beliefs. Also, as a family, we do not accept drug dealing. Drug dealing is equivalent to second-degree murder. Your son will, over time, buy into your family's beliefs, morals, and values. This will help your child make choices that align with the family's belief system and resist peer pressure.

15 TIPS FOR RAISING A CHILD'S SELF-ESTEEM

1. Reward children.
    a. Give praise, recognition, a special privilege, or increased responsibility for a job well done.
    b. Emphasize the good things they do, not just what they do wrong.
    c. Catch the child in the act of being good.

2. Take their ideas, emotions, and feelings seriously.
    a. Don't belittle them by saying: "You'll grow out of it!" or "It's not as bad as you think."

3. Define limits and rules clearly and enforce them.
    a. Do allow leeway for your children within these limits.

4. Be a good role model.
    a. Let your child know that you feel good about yourself.
    b. Let them see that you too can make mistakes and

    learn from those mistakes.
  c. Tell your child about your experiences.

5. Teach your children how to deal with time and money.
   a. Help them spend time wisely and budget their money carefully.

6. Have reasonable expectations for your children.
   a. Help them to set reachable goals so they can achieve success.

7. Help the child develop tolerance of others with different values and norms.
   a. Point out other people's strengths.

8. Give your children responsibility.
   a. Your child will feel useful and valued.

9. Be available.
   a. Give support when children need it.
   b. Drop something important to you and respond to your child's needs.

10. Show them that what they do is important to you.
    a. Talk with them about their activities and interests.
    b. Go to their games, Parent's Day, plays, and awards ceremonies.

11. Express your values but go beyond "do this" or "I want

you to do that."
   a. Describe the experiences that determined your values, the decisions you made to accept certain beliefs and the reasons behind your feelings.

12. Spend time together.
    a. Share favorite activities.

13. Discuss problems without placing blame or commenting on their character.
    a. If children know that there is a problem but don't feel attacked, they are more likely to help look for a solution.

14. Use phrases that build self-esteem, such as "Thank you for helping" or "That was an excellent idea!"
    a. Avoid phrases that hurt self-esteem "Why are you so stupid?" or "How many times have I told you?"

15. Show how much you care about them.
    a. Hug them.
    b. Tell them they are terrific and that you love them.

Source: National PTA

BLACK BOYS LACKING SELF-DISCIPLINE

"FAIL EARLY,
FAIL OFTEN,
FAIL FORWARD"
JOHN C. MAXWELL

Research shows, Black Boys who grow up in fatherless households are more likely to act out in school and to use drugs. They are also more likely to suffer from low self-esteem, depression, and other mental illnesses. Many Black Boys come to school without adequate social skills to function in a classroom environment. These males are confronted with two "selves": the "one-self," which depicts what community and peers expect of them, and the "other-self," what the school expects of them (Bell, 2010; Bell, 2009). When Black Boys cannot bring the two selves together, the one-self emerges when it is time to enter the school building. Common courtesy, raising hands, active listening, being self-disciplined, being prepared, and waiting their turn are only a few of the needed social skills Black Boys must possess and display in today's classrooms (Bell, 2010b; Bell, 2009). As simplistic as these may sound, these traits must be internalized by Black Boys. When these skills are not developed at home or in the community, it becomes difficult for Black Boys to transfer those skills into the school environment. Majors and Billson (1992) concluded that Black Boys' behavior is often misinterpreted. Misinterpretation can cause educators to conclude that Black Boys are innately rude and have an aversion towards schooling (Majors and Billson, 1992).

The culture of learning in most schools comes with expectations. Many Black Boys must come to appreciate school for its primary purpose; a place to learn. Good and Brophy (1995) discussed factors that teachers can implement to teach social learning, such as addressing realistic perceptions of students while concomitantly enjoying teaching. Teachers must present clear and consistent roles and respond to a crisis in a fair and equitable manner. African American males must be taught how to survive in today's classrooms (Bell, 2010a). Raising African American males can be a challenging pursuit in a world that tends to undervalue the culture and achievements of this population (Hare and Hare, 1991; Bell, 2009; Douglass, 2007).

DEVELOPING SELF-DISCIPLINE IN BLACK BOYS

1. The following strategies can impact learning for Black Boys:
   - Focus on sharpening and broadening communication skills ("Obama" style).
   - Develop creative ways to channel potentially self-destructive emotions.
   - Model appropriate social skills and self-discipline.
   - Have the boys see and interact with Black men who are positive models.
   - Just listen to what they have to say to help them to critically think about what they are saying and how it can affect their future.
   - Explain the reason behind the rules. Understanding the rules can help the boy make healthy choices.

2. Steps to teaching self-discipline:

STEP 1 – START EARLY

It is always easiest to teach young minds because they are very impressionable. My grandmother, born in 1890, could not read or write' told me this analogy. Take two acorns and plant both at the same time. Let one grow for six months, and let the other grow for six years. At the end of each growth period, go back and pull it up from the ground. The one at six months is easily pulled up but the one that has been in the ground for six years, you need a block and tackle to get it out of the ground. She said behavior is the same way, the longer you allow it to grow, the harder it is to pull it out of you. The earlier you start teaching a child, the easier it is for them to follow directions because their minds are like blank canvasses. Start with simple things like coming as soon as they are called and regularly reinforcing the use of "Please," "Thank you," and "Excuse Me." Simple chores like packing away their toys after playtime, making their beds in the morning, and always keeping their rooms neat.

STEP 2 – HAVE ROUTINES

Repetition and routine structure are critical in every child's daily life. It may seem boring for adults, but children depend on it. It gives them a feeling of security knowing what is supposed to happen next. Set a daily schedule for them from the time they wake up until the time they need to go to sleep. I taught kids with behavior problems, and it was much easier for them when I kept a daily routine for them; they became self-disciplined and followed the schedule every day without being told to do so.

STEP 3 – TAKE CORRECTIONS POSITIVELY

Most boys do not react to being corrected well. They respond with a bad attitude or become very angry. This would be a good time to start teaching what self-discipline is about. Teaching that life is full of ups and downs, that some time you win, and sometimes you lose is pertinent. They must learn that either way they must learn to stay in control of themselves. Also, they have to learn that when they make a mistake, they must deal with it by trying to correct the mistake rather than acting out. It is all about controlling their feelings and impulses. Let them know that they are human, and we all make mistakes and instead of getting upset, they should learn from it.

STEP 4 – ENCOURAGE DISCIPLINED ACTIVITIES

Playing board games and video games can teach discipline. There are rules to all these games that you must follow in order to play the games. Using those concepts found in the games allow transferring those behaviors to their everyday walk of life. Organized athletics like basketball, football, martial arts, or other sports, and activities such as music, camping or fishing can help develop self-discipline in these boys and increase their self-assurance. It gives them a sense of accomplishment when they move on to the next level.

STEP 5 – HAVE RULES

You must set very clear rules at home and be consistent about following the rules as well as applying consequences when they break the rules. This is a way to teach the boys what to expect if they follow the rules or not; it will also help him make better decisions.

STEP 6 – UNDERSTAND THAT LEARNING SELF-DISCIPLINE IS DIFFICULT

Let the boy know that you understand that learning to become self-disciplined can be difficult. Then tell them that you also know how strong and smart they are, and that is why they will be able to accomplish them just by trying hard enough.

STEP 7 – HAVE PRAISE AND REWARDS

Praise and rewards (hugs, time with the child, etc.) for good behavior go much further as a form of discipline than punishment. Simply giving the child positive attention and respect when he is not misbehaving will act as an extremely strong reinforcer for good behavior. Give praise, recognition, a special privilege or increased responsibility for a job well done. Emphasize the good things they do, not just the negative things. Catch the boy in the act of being good and praise the behavior not the child. This is being done to bolster the child's effort to continue this behavior. I remember seeing a television commercial when a kid ran into the house hollering," Dad, Dad, I got an A in class today!" But the dad responded, "Didn't I tell you not to slam that door!" The dad missed an opportunity to catch his son in the act of doing something good. This was an opportunity to employ praise to reinforce discipline. The father should understand that praise can build healthy self-esteem when he points out the effort the son has put forth to earn an A.

OLD SCHOOL BLACK MOMS GOT IT RIGHT

RESPECT YOURSELF

"THE MOST EXPENSIVE THING IN THE WORLD IS TRUST. IT CAN TAKE YEARS TO EARN AND JUST A MATTER OF SECONDS TO LOSE"

TUPAC SHAKUR

BLACK BOYS DEVELOPING SELF-RESPECT

Self-respect is pride and confidence in oneself; a feeling that one behaves with honor and dignity. Here are some steps parents can use to teach self-respect:

1. **Set the standards of respect for in and out of the home.**

    Explain to your son early in life and continue through his growth and development that respect is a family value. That he is expected to respect everyone in the house, other adults, people in charge of him at school and the community, as well as, his peers. Early on, start using and defining terms such as respect, disrespect, polite, and rude to develop a common language of respect.

2. **Tune your ears to the sound of respect and disrespect.**

    You must start tuning in on not just what they say but how they say it (interruptions, accusations, name calling, tone of voice, etc.). Pay attention when the boy is using words that are attacking, intrusive, sarcastic, and mean.

3. **Nip disrespectful behavior in the bud.**

    Respond immediately when the boy is being disrespectful. Let him know that this behavior is unacceptable and goes against your family's values.

4. **Use a special tone of voice and facial expressions in response to disrespect.**

    This special voice and facial expressions communicate to the boy that he is treading in dangerous territory. It tells him to check himself before he wrecks himself.

5. **Be firm, but keep your cool.**

    When you stay cool in any situation, you are modeling self-discipline. Also, you show him you are a confident parent when you display that you are calm, clear, focused, and assertive in times of conflict.

6. **Challenge every disrespectful behavior.**

    Showing repetitive behavior when he is displaying disrespectful behavior lets him know that you mean business. He will understand that you expect him not to behave in that fashion. Ensure you stay the course and over time, the negative behavior will cease.

We must teach Black Boys that they are the most important person in their lives. We often focus on the concepts of sharing and thinking of the other person first, but there is merit in allowing boys to meet their own needs first and then considering the needs of others. Sensitivity to others occurs naturally without prompting after we have taken care of ourselves. Some may perceive this approach as selfish, but does it not stand to reason that we are better able to serve others after we have made sure that we are whole?

WE MUST ALSO TEACH BLACK BOYS ABOUT BOUNDARIES

1. First and foremost, these boundaries include teaching how to protect their physical and emotional health. Your boy needs to learn emphatically that no one has the right to jeopardize their physical or emotional safety.

2. Secondly, explain to your son that just as it makes sense to say yes at times, it is also socially acceptable to say no at other times. Just as it's fine to spend lots of time with a friend during the week, it's equally OK to spend less time with the same friend when that friend is being too demanding or needy.

3. And finally, like with many other lessons passed on from parents to children, teaching children about healthy boundaries is easier when parents can do so by example. Take stock of your own personal boundaries and do an honest assessment. Healthy boundaries often require us to be confident in our own opinions, desires, and needs. To build that confidence, children need to learn how to

identify what they need, where their limits are, and the types of interactions with which they are comfortable.

Teach your sons respect for others by modeling respect for others in your words and actions, especially in how you interact with others in your house. The dynamics in your home have a powerful influence on your children. The Golden Rule is a perfect example of how we should conduct ourselves. It is a general rule for how to behave that says you should treat people the way you would like others to treat you.

BLACK BOYS SELF-FULFILLMENT OF DREAMS (SELF-REALIZATION)

Self-fulfillment means the realization or achievement of one's goals and potentialities. Those old school Black Moms worked hard to make their sons understand that their dreams were not silly or stupid. They would tell them that their dreams were very important to them. These moms knew that their son's dreams would help make them become successful men in the future.

Those old school Black Moms would not allow their

sons to not have a purpose in life. By constantly talking about their dreams, they would be planted in the deepest part of their mind, their subconscious. Serious dreams can come true. They never allowed their sons to give up on the dreams they showed a lot of interest in.

THEY TAUGHT THEIR SONS THE FIVE W'S FOR GOAL ORGANIZING:

1. What is my goal?
2. Who will help me reach my goal?
3. Where will I work on my goal?
4. When will I achieve my goal?
5. Why is this goal important to me?

They had them write down, and read them every day.
1. Every thought they had about their dreams.
2. All the people they might need to make their dreams come true.
3. What steps they must take to make their dreams come true.

They worked on things they needed to improve, and sometimes they had to change or update a goal.
1. They taught their sons rather than being fearful of things that are different or unknown, they must discern life as it unfolds both logically and rationally.
2. These boys are often motivated by a strong sense of personal ethics and responsibility.

3. They were taught problem-solving skills using real-world situations.
4. Their friendships with others could often cause them to not take time for themselves. However, taking time for themselves would allow for personal discovery and cultivating their individual potential.
5. They would see the attempt to complete their goal as a journey, not just the destination.

The use of high self-esteem, self-respect, and their belief in God allowed these boys to see the possibility of bringing their dreams to fruition. These moms had high expectations of their sons through all phases of their development. They taught them early on that being confident, working hard, and being dedicated to their dreams would cause success.

EMPOWERING BLACK BOYS TO WORK THROUGH THEIR SELF-CRISIS

There are no easy answers to the trials these young men will face in life. However, by empowering them to utilize science-based social skill strategies, they can obtain knowledge that can help change many negative behaviors as they progress into manhood. This positive progression in the lives of young men will help them avoid the pitfall of a self-crisis. Also, they can avoid many mistakes that cause their involvement in both the juvenile and adult justice systems. When I speak of both juvenile and adult justice systems, I am talking about the knowledge they can obtain that will create public safety in our communities. This public safety happens when they are taught how to react with acceptable social norms, when they are able to curb their fascination with guns, when they see the need for formal education, as well as the need to learn good morals, ethics, and values.

The Youth Exposed to Success (YES) Program was an outreach program I conducted in the metropolitan Washington, DC area in the 1980's and 1990's. This was the period when DC was the murder capital of the United States. The YES Program provided interventions that addressed the self-crisis that most of these fatherless Black Boys were immersed in. The YES, Program had a clear vision with specific, targeted outcomes intended for the intervention of these Black Boys. The program provided skill-building activities that enabled these young men to successfully make the transition to adulthood. The ultimate goal was that these young Black Boys would become productive and engaged adult citizens. This creates law-abiding boys, connected to meaningful work, in healthy relationships, and living in healthy environments.

The Youth Exposed to Success program specialized in addressing issues related to these self-crises. How to project a positive self-image, building positive self-esteem, how to self-discipline themselves, how to respect themselves and others and how to self-actualize their dreams and goals.

These self-crises were occurring in many of these at-risk boys of color. The YES Program utilized its scientific-based social skill curriculum and hands-on application concentrated on skill building. These skills focus on teaching a balance in social, emotional, physical, spiritual, and psychological skills to redirect negative energy toward positive patterns. This program had phenomenal success. Most of the YES Program participants have a trade or college degree. Most are fathers living with their children and are law-abiding citizens who made that successful transition to adulthood. The strategies the YES program utilized to address a balance in social, emotional, physical, spiritual, and psychological were as follows:

STRATEGIES

The YES Program set up programmatic efforts to get participants involved in mainstream activities that would teach participants how to accept and utilize societal norms.

1. **Socially**

Many of the YES Program participants lacked social balance and the ability to interact successfully by utilizing societal norms in their community. Some of the negative behaviors they displayed caused conflict with peers and adults, poor relationships with teachers, risky sexual behavior, substance abuse, and the sale of illegal substances. Those negative behaviors also resulted in poor communication skills, not developing intimacy with others, and finally, not creating a support network of friends and family members (the village).

a. Afterschool Programs

A free program for low-income middle school students at their school five days a week. This program was designed to boost attendance during the school day, raise graduation rates, improve gains in reading and math proficiency, and enhance engagement in school. It lowered behavioral issues and increased the likelihood of taking college preparatory courses. I observed that students who engaged consistently in the after-school programs did not experiment with drugs, alcohol, or criminal behavior; behavior/referrals and academic performance improved by more than 50 percent.

b. Dance Parties

African American vernacular dance: Core culture and meaning operatives cited that during the early adolescent years, the dance is a significant socialization mechanism, particularly for Black urban youth. The Outreach Program held Friday dance parties for the kids in the community. Every Friday at the Middle School, we would hold these dances for teens ages 13-17 to promote positive youth development through a specially designed dance party by teens and for teens. This teen night was from 7 pm to 10 pm. This activity included a DJ playing the latest hits and a concession stand. All of the participants were forewarned that drugs or alcohol were not allowed. The purpose was to reduce idleness among teenagers and help them stay out of trouble by socializing with their friends, both males and females. Our aim was to give the kids a safe environment to hang out in with adult supervision on Friday nights. With this activity, we were able to show our participants how to behave appropriately and positively in a social setting. Hazzard-Gordon, K. (1985) (Journal of Black Studies, 1985)

c. **Midnight Basketball**

Midnight Basketball was a program for at-risk urban youth used to curb crime and delinquency and create public safety. Our Midnight Basketball League was created to help reduce crime rates in our community. It created a safe haven in which participants for both players and spectators could engage in positive social activities. It presented an opportunity to channel any negative energy in a positive direction, and help improve the educational and career aspirations of program participants.

The Midnight Basketball League was structured where teens were able to set up their individual teams (players had to be between the ages of 13 to 17 and not playing for a school team). We accepted the first eight teams to register. We set up an eight-game season with the top four teams competing in the playoffs. Every two weeks, we would hold a workshop that included sessions on Gang Violence (week

2), Policemen: Friend or Foe (week 4), Substance Abuse: Use, Abuse and Sell (week 6), and Vocational Opportunities in Various Trades (week 8). The rule was each player from each team had to register and attend each workshop or they could not play in league's game for the next two weeks. An empirical study conducted on midnight basketball as a crime prevention strategy entitled "Rethinking Sports-Based Community Crime Prevention." The authors conducted a preliminary empirical test of the claim, dismissed by most scholars, that midnight basketball programs lowered city-level crime rates. The results showed cities that were early adopters of officially sanctioned midnight basketball leagues experienced sharper decreases in property crime rates than other American cities during a period of broad support for midnight basketball programs (Hartmann & Depro, 2006). Don Terry, in his New York Article "Basketball at Midnight: 'Hope' on a Summer Eve," said that the program helps show the young men a sense of community, friendship, and sportsmanship that they wouldn't have gotten to experience on the streets (Terry, 1994). With this activity, we were able to accomplish our goal of creating a safe haven, reducing crime in our community, and giving our participants much needed career information.

d. Work Programs

The YES Program's work component consisted of a lawn service where, depending on the season, they would cut grass, rake leave, shovel snow or do odd jobs for community residents. The program provided all of the equipment needed to complete the work. Staff would advertise the program services to the community. In turn, the residents would arrange with staff for program participants to provide the services requested. The boys would be assigned a job that would be performed on evenings and Saturdays. If there were residents for whom the program provided services on a regular basis, the same boy would be assigned to that person. In addition to earning money for the jobs they completed, they also learned work ethics. Those work ethics included:

1) They were taught to value time and practice punctuality - They were given a time frame for completing a job, and if they did not adhere to those times, their pay could be docked. If they were late coming to their assigned pick-up area, their job was given to someone else.
2) They would suffer the consequences of failing to work hard – If they did not complete the assigned work at that expected level, their pay could be docked, and they would not receive an assignment for the following week.
3) We worked on building good character - They were left alone to complete an assigned task. They had to be self-disciplined to carry out the job in an excellent manner. This built character and good character is key to a good work ethic. That type of determination,

motivation, and self-confidence pushed them to do good work.

4) We provided motivation to continue doing good work - Staff would acknowledge their achievements whether small or big when a task was completed. They were complimented on a job well done.

2. Emotionally

The lack of emotional balance is when human emotions such as happiness, sadness, rage, depression, and anger are expressed incorrectly. The rage, or anger, described in the quote by James Baldwin, "To be a Negro in this country and to be relatively conscious is to be in a rage almost all the time." It is often a secondary emotion accompanied by primary emotions such as rejection, humiliation, and sadness. This lack of balance has created the inability for self-acceptance. A lack of self-acceptance has come about by either not recognizing or lacking the skills to address historical trauma in their lives. These forms of trauma include destruction of cultural practices, slavery, forced relocation, genocide, and police brutality among others, and can deeply impact individuals, families, and entire communities.

a. Peer counseling program

For eight consecutive years, fifteen youth received 25 hours of peer counseling and training from a master's level mental health counselor. The peer counselors learned important life skills, giving them the ability to help their peers work through many crises. They learned confidentiality, listening skills, problem-solving skills, suicide prevention, bullying, how to deal with stress, coping skills, grief, and conflict resolution. While completing the training, the peer counselors would direct the content of peer-run and peer-governed bi-weekly meetings. Each peer counselor was responsible for bringing two individuals to participate in the bi-weekly forums. This would bring each meeting to a minimum of 45 participants per session. The youth were very open and helpful with one another.

The youths suggested topics for meetings, which are overseen by a trained peer facilitator. The peer counselors became active Listeners. They allowed their peers to talk while they listened attentively, they did not offer information or try to immediately solve a problem. The process involved empathy, being nonjudgmental, asking open-ended questions, being understanding, and practicing exploration. Sometimes, the group would invite presenters to talk about such issues as substance abuse, stress, domestic violence, and anger.

3. Physically

The lack of physical balance is the need to implement proper nutrition and abstain from harmful habits such as risky sexual behavior, drug use, and alcohol abuse. They have problems identifying symptoms of disease, not getting regular medical checkups, or protecting themselves from injuries and harm.

a. Open gym programs

Local school gyms were open twice a week to play basketball and other physical activities at no cost. These activities had a positive effect on many risk factors, such as increased self-esteem, increased well-being, and increased acquisition of "life skills." For example, participants demonstrated better goal setting and planning abilities, increased values development and lowered substance abuse and criminal behavior.

b. Summer Basketball Leagues

The YES Program's Summer Basketball League instilled lifelong lessons. These lessons helped our participants learn to work together, build relationships and play with others. These boys underwent a transformation from feeling alone to understanding that they were part of a team. Often, for many of them, this was their first time experiencing self-worth and self-confidence. The Summer Basketball League was designed to allow the high school participants to run the leagues. The high school students were the coaches, scorekeepers, and referees. Over an eight-year period, these young men learned leadership skills, teamwork, problem solving, adaptability, and communication. They also gained the ability to plan, prioritize, and use time management skills. The league players were made up of our elementary and middle school participants. They learned individual and team skills, how to take pride in themselves, and how to set personal and team goals. The players also learned how to measure progress through effort, commitment, responsibility and, taking genuine pride in their accomplishments.

4. Spiritually

The lack of spiritual balance is when they need to possess a set of guiding beliefs, principles, or values that help give direction to their life. They do not have a high level of faith, hope, and commitment to their individual beliefs that provide a sense of meaning and purpose.

a. Taught Volunteerism

Teaching these boys volunteerism was valuable in shaping how they learned to interact with their community, developed principles, and felt the sense of meaning and purpose necessary to become productive citizens. They would keep saying, "this is our way of giving back to the community." The projects our participants helped with were passing out city newsletters, Thanksgiving and Christmas food giveaways, helping senior citizens, and hosting fundraisers for a variety of community needs. Volunteering also allowed the opportunity to teach teens how to network and build a list of important contacts.

5. **Psychologically**

The lack of psychological balance is when the ability to be creative and participate in stimulating mental activities in a positive manner is absent. Individuals who lack psychological balance do not use the resources available to expand one's knowledge and improve their decision-making skills. When young Black Boys do not know their life's purpose and how to self-actualize it as they mature into adulthood, they will continually make mistakes that get them into all kinds of trouble. As stated in 1 Corinthians 13:11, "When I was a child, I spake as a child, I understood as a child, I thought as a child: but when I became a man, I put away childish things." Those childish things that were not put away created this self-crisis. This model includes skill building in areas of:
- Self-Image – How do I see myself?
- Self-Esteem – How do I feel about myself?
- Self-Discipline – Am I in control of myself?
- Self-Respect – Do I bring honor to myself?
- Self-Actualization – How am I maximizing my potential?

a. **Teen Altering Behavior of Self (T.A.B.S.) Program**

The YES Program conducted the T.A.B.S. Program curriculum, which was an 8-week class of behavior modification instruction two days per week for 1 hour each session. The purpose of the T.A.B.S. curriculum was to give our target population a workable option to change their anti-social behavior and redirect negative energies toward positive patterns. It was the program's objective that through the course curriculum, the participants would be able to integrate practical positive conduct to start understanding their life's purpose and how to self-actualize it as they mature into adulthood.

The behavior techniques taught during the sessions were as follows:

- Adolescent Substance Abuse Intervention
- Rewards and consequences of your behavior
- Coping, Decision Making & Problem-Solving Skills
- The Youth Cognitive Life Skills
- Life Skills for Gang Intervention
- Goal Setting Skills

b. Trips (camping, amusement parks, cultural museums)

These trips were activities outside of school that were designed to be associated with adaptive and positive personal development for our participants. These activities provided support and a means for socialization and the acquisition of social skills while increasing their sense of belonging. These activities helped to reduce tension through involvement in positive activities outside of their normal environment. Engaging in out-of-school activities is also linked to an increased sense of achievement and to higher levels of self-esteem (Still, 2013). These types of activities provided opportunities for exposure to other lifestyles and social networks as well as opportunities for experiential learning (Still, 2013). We found that these activities were critical to their growth and development.

CHAPTER 7

OLD SCHOOL BLACK MOMS GOT IT RIGHT

OLD SCHOOL BLACK MOMS GOT IT RIGHT

Black Moms from the 50's, 60's, and 70's understood a few things missing from the toolbox of our modern-day Black Moms. They came with a bible and a belt. I will explain this analogy later in this section. The first thing they understood was that they were not their child's friend; they were their parent. In fact, many of those moms would literally tell their sons, "I'm not one of your little friends." They did not allow their child to fool them by telling them something that did not make sense or thinking that they were stupid, saying, "Do I look like booboo the fool?" They did not allow them to talk to them as if they were adults too. They would tell that boy something like, "Don't let your mouth write a check your ass can't cash." They always took the role of being in charge. Another familiar phrase that would be echoed by mothers of that generation is, "I don't care what John's mama does. I'm not John's mama." They would always tell them what the right thing for them was, and not just one time. "You are my child, and I am gonna tell you what you may and may not do; and if you have a problem with me telling you what you can and can't do, let the doorknob hit you where the good Lord split you." This meant if they did not follow the instructions given, they could look to be punished for their actions, potentially leading to ultimately having to be put out of the house. They did not allow them to talk in a disrespectful ton. They would say, "first of all, check your tone."

They did not teach them how to be emotional. One of the things they would tell them is, "You better stop all that crying before I give you something to cry about." They would say, "Don't you get in trouble following behind those good-time friends of yours in the street." They knew all your friends, most of their parents, and where they lived. They would tell them, "I don't care what they do at their house. You live in this house, and this is what we do here." Not only did the Black Moms from the 50's, 60's and 70's have these sayings, they also followed up on everything they said. They were consistent in their discipline. The child meant more to them than a man, the streets, a party, or being able to do their own thing. They understood that a child spelled LOVE – with T-I-M-E. These mothers knew that they had to spend a lot of time with their child. Also, they knew they had to model the behavior they wanted their child to display. They not only taught, but they showed them what was expected of them.

Old school Black Moms taught their sons that they had to put themselves first. They are the most important person in their own lives. They made sure they understood that being sensitive to others occurs naturally, but they have to take care of themselves before helping others. Some may perceive this approach as selfish; however, doesn't it stand to reason that we are better able to serve others after we have made sure that we are whole? An example of this idea would be if a child has a playmate coming to visit and has a special toy he or she doesn't want to share. The child can put away that toy, and other toys can be chosen to share. That tells your child that it is okay to meet his or her own needs, and that message that will serve him or her well throughout life.

Old school Black Moms believed in the African proverb, "It takes a village to raise a child," which means that an entire community of people must interact with children for those children to experience growth in a safe and healthy environment. Because many of these Black Moms were either working parents and also single parents trying to raise a family, it took the support of a "village" for their children to grow up in a safe and healthy environment. The village consisted of adults, outside of the nuclear family, who played an important role in the boy's life. Coaches, teachers, aunts, uncles, family friends, and grandparents used to pick up the slack when parents were unable.

The segregated school system was a very big part of the Black community's village, even though their school's educational opportunities were unequal. Black teachers were often paid less than their counterparts in white schools, and they taught with outdated textbooks that were handed down from the white schools in the district. Some of the black school buildings were crumbling, with inadequate heating and cooling systems (Will, 2019). In this so-called separate but equal system, there were many more blatant inequalities. Yet it is still my belief that the integration of public schools hurt Black children more than it helped. Inside the classrooms of those segregated schools, there was a focus on civics and democratic ideals. Black children were taught to aspire to greater things than the status quo of segregation (Will, 2019). They were taught that they had to do better than the white students, so when they were not afforded equal chances, they would still be a step ahead to qualify anyway. In these schools, strong interpersonal relationships between teachers and black students were formed. On a personal note, I can remember my first year in high school in 1966. I gave my homeroom teacher my projected class schedule. She told me she had read my cumulative folder and she could tell that I was college material, so she would make my class schedule for me. I did not have any idea I would attend college. Not only did I attend college, but I have earned a Doctoral degree. I must also give credit to all my instructors because I graduated from a segregated setting with only Black teachers who taught with substandard materials. Nevertheless, I was able to attend all-white colleges and did excellently, thanks to those Black teachers who prepared me well. And finally, the shift from segregation in the public school system caused Black Boys to lose a very important component to them becoming productive Black Men. Many of those teachers were Black males who helped redirect those Black Boys negative energies toward positive patterns. They were Black role models and mentors for many boys who did not have fathers in their homes. They showed them how to become good husbands and fathers and taught them good work ethics so they could become exceptional, productive citizens.

NEW SCHOOL BLACK MOM TOOLBOX FOR RAISING BLACK BOYS

1. Faith In Something Greater Than Oneself

Many old school Black Mothers believed in a power greater than themselves. In other words, they believed there was a God, and His word had to be followed. This belief also said that you had a greater purpose in life than just having a good time while on earth. These Black Women believed they had an alliance with God where God reacted to their faith by blessing them because of what His word says: "you reap what you sow," both now and in the afterlife. So, if you give and help others, God will meet your needs. They regarded God as a personal friend who has an intimate relationship with them. This faith caused them to believe that peace begins and ends with God's authority, which means the key to living a life of joy, peace, and happiness is to have faith in God. This relationship with God caused them not to be scared of anything. They believed that if they trusted and were guided by the Lord, they could face any situation that came their way. At the end of the day, their faith centered on Philippians 4:13, which says, "I can do all things through Christ who strengthens me." The Word of God was their hiding place and shield for their son. As the old hymn goes: "If I hold my peace and let the Lord fight my battles, Victory, victory shall be mine." Most of the boys didn't understand this concept as children, but as they became adults, they came to understand what their moms were telling them.

2. Communicating Family Values

The old school Black Mom did not assume their sons knew or understood their family values. They knew it was their responsibility to communicate their family morals and values to their sons. They also told their son, that as a member of the family, they are expected to abide by all of those values. When they communicated these family morals and values, they were very specific and clear. Not only did they tell their son, which is a form of teaching, but they also modeled the desired behavior for the child. They modeled and taught that there were certain types of behaviors that their family would not accept. Those moms told them what it was and showed them what it looked like, calling the subject exactly what it was. If you were speaking about oral sex, then that was stated. They did not beat around the bush. They did not tell and show them once and expect them to remember; this was an ongoing conversation throughout the child's life. These mothers stayed a couple of stages (one to two years) ahead of the child's development by giving them information in advance. They did it to have a long-term effect on the child. So, over time, these boys bought into their family beliefs, morals, and values. When it was time for the boy to make life decisions, his choices lined up with the family's belief system and gave him a better chance of resisting peer pressure.

3. Rules Used to Discipline a Black Boy

Although many Black Moms believed in some of the teachings that favors discussion and understanding before punishment takes place, many of them unquestionably are a believer in old school principles. These principles were a rewards and punishments system intended to change negative behavior to positive behavior. These mothers would reward their sons for good behavior and punish them for poor behavior. The mother ruled her house with an iron fist. They stood on the old adage, "My way or the highway." They also believed in tough love; sometimes you had to give them a spanking and tell them, "This is going to hurt me more that it will hurt you." They often told them, "No, doesn't mean I don't love you; it means I know what is better for you than you do." These moms would let the son know the rules were set, and you would follow them to the "T." Old school Black Moms believed in black and white, and there was no gray area. When they set the rules; the punishments were consistent. It was understood that they were the parent, and the child was not in charge of anything.

RULE 1: DISCIPLINE DOES NOT START AFTER THEY HAVE GOTTEN INTO TROUBLE

Oftentimes, many Black Moms wait until an incident occurs before they begin the act of disciplining their son. This is the definition of discipline we will use: the practice of training a person to obey rules or a code of behavior. Old school Black Moms understood that you are not to just focus on the obedience part and forget the training part. These old school Black Moms recognized that if they wanted their son to behave in a certain manner, they must be trained to do so. That means if you want your son to be respectful to all adults, they'll have to practice it consistently with all the adults in their life. This training was done all day while with their son.

RULE 2: 80% IS OKAY!

These old school Black Moms also understood if the boy completed 80% of the task well, they would praise the boy for a job well done. They wanted to catch them in the act of doing good so they could praise the behavior and get them to keep working at it. They also let them know they would not be the first person in the world to have made a mistake. They helped their boy understand that it was better to make a mistake while they were young because the tears they shed as a kid are not the same tears they will shed as an adult, nor are the consequences they will experience even if it was for the same mistake. This allowed them to check themselves before they wrecked themselves as adults.

RULE 3: BOYS NEED A DAILY SCHEDULE

These old school Black Moms gave their sons age-appropriate daily schedules. This schedule included being on time for all activities, and their daily chores. They were assigned at least 2-3 chores daily and were expected to complete them in a timely manner. As long as they followed the schedule, there was not any trouble, but if they did not complete the chores or were not on time, they would face some type of consequence. They ingrained self-discipline in their sons by being repetitive and consistent when applying schedules, chores, and consequences. This taught their son where the boundaries were. They worked hard on ensuring that their expectations for their sons were clearly laid out, not by just following the rules, but by how they engaged with their sons on a daily basis.

OLD SCHOOL BLACK MOMS CAME WITH A BIBLE & A BELT

Old school Black Moms came with a bible and a belt as means of rearing their children. The Bible and a belt had a deeper meaning than what you see on the surface.

- The Bible represented the picture of God as our shepherd, and we are the sheep of his pasture. He is to guide and lead us in the right way to go. This is what old school Black Moms became for their boys. The boys were their sheep, and they were the shepherd. It was their job to keep them on the right track, so they would not go astray. And if they did go astray, they were there to pull them back in line. This tight reign helped these boys grow up to become great and awesome men.

- In this book the Belt is an analogy for the rod that is found in the Bible. We are using the bible verse Proverbs 13:24 NIV - "Whoever spares the rod hates their children, but the one who loves their children is careful to discipline them." This belt/rod does not mean just spanking and hitting the child; it also is speaking of setting boundaries and giving logical consequences. In the Bible the rod was constantly in the shepherd's hand as he walked in front of the sheep and led the way. When the sheep started to stray in directions that could lead to trouble, the shepherd would use the rod to redirect them to safety.

THE BIBLE

The Bible is used by Christians to give them guidance about how they can live their lives in the way God instructs them to. There is guidance in the Bible on many areas of life and Christians will turn to this advice when they are faced with a dilemma. Old school Black Moms used God's Word that instructed them to "train up our children in the way they should go." They understood that they had to use God's strength and wisdom to raise their sons. Also, many of these moms followed Proverbs 23:13 MSG "Don't be afraid to correct your young ones; a spanking won't kill them." These moms used the answers found in Proverbs 3:5-6, "Trust in the LORD with all your heart, and lean not on your own understanding; In all your ways acknowledge him, and he will direct your path".

These old school Black Moms used the Bible to give guidance and direction to their sons during their growth and devolvement period. They taught their son good morals, values, ethics, and generally how to live a life according to their family values and societal norms, which usually came from the Bible. With this guidance, the boy would learn self-disciple, self-control, high self-esteem, positive self-worth, and self-respect that would help them become productive adults. Learning these techniques prepared them to make good decisions when faced with life's dilemmas.

They made sure they let their sons know that they were not a mistake, that they are the likeness of God and are unique among His creation.

- They knew that one of the most powerful ways to show love to their child was to be consistent in how they discipline them. And sometimes it was really hard. They were not trying to be their child's, friend they were to be their parent. Recognizing as a parent, it was more important to discipline them rather forming a friendship, which was not always easy.

- They understood that they could not discipline well for a few weeks, and then find it more convenient to make compromises. They had to be consistent because they knew their sons would realize that they would eventually give in and see that these were just empty threats, these moms had to follow through.

The Black Mom knew that respect was an essential moral value that their sons must know about at a young age. Respect plays an important role in his behavior around strangers and elders. When they taught their toddlers to learn how to respect their peers and elders from a young age, it benefited them as they grew and developed into adulthood.

Biblical **STEPS** Old School Black Moms used to raise their sons.

STEP – 1: MODEL & TEACH

Using Proverbs 22:6 – "Train up a child in the way he should go: and when he is old, he will not depart from it." These mothers gave daily tasks and expected for them to be accomplished in an efficient and timely manner. Giving boys chores is a way to make them feel significant or needed because they are able to contribute to the family. These daily tasks included making up their bed before leaving for school, cleaning up the kitchen, sweeping the floors, etc. They expected these chores to be accomplished when they got home from work. I remember when I was a kid, my mother instilled in me and my brothers and sisters, "thou shall not steal." She was very tough on us about it. I would have rather put-on gasoline underwear and walk-through hell than let her catch me with something stolen. This ethical standard is a part of me as an adult. I will not even take a pencil or a pad from the job because I see it as taking something that does not belong to me. As parents they would model good behavior and understood that this training provided was to continue until they became adults.

STEP – 2: THESE MOMS LEAD BY EXAMPLE

They followed Titus 2:7, "Show yourself in all respects to be a model of good works, and in your teaching show integrity and dignity." They understood that their sons looked up to them and paid close attention to them to see if their behavior was worthy of imitation. They knew if they constantly yelled and screamed at others or treated people with no respect, their sons would do the same. As children get older, they have many relationships outside the home, so these moms wanted their son's behavior to reflect the family values modeled at home. Leading by example was all about getting their sons to imitate the behavior that they had seen their moms use in and outside the house. They knew that if the boys saw them acting badly, they would raise sons that behaved badly as well.

STEP – 3: THEY HELP THEIR SONS PREPARE FOR THE FUTURE AND START SETTING GOALS

The used Jeremiah 29:11, which says, "For I know the plans I have for you," declares the Lord, "plans to prosper you and not to harm you, plans to give you hope and a future." They continually asked them what they wanted to be, knowing most likely, it would change a million times as they grew up. However, asking this question enables the child to start developing a vision of themselves in the future. They knew it was important to follow up this question with questions about how they could make it happen, such as: "So you want to be an airplane mechanic, what kind of effort do you think you should put towards your math homework to do this type of work? It was understood that these kinds of questions would cause the boy to not just think about the dream, but also consider the effort it would take to accomplish his dream. This type of thinking would cause him to begin putting his dream into action.

STEP – 4: THEY WORKED ON CHARACTER BUILDING

These moms used 1 Timothy 4:12, which says, "Don't let anyone look down on you because you are young, but set an example for the believers in speech, in conduct, in love, in faith and in purity." These moms would use teachable moments to build character. They understood that their sons could learn that when they violate the family's values and ethics that the appropriate consequences would be applied. They had a strategy to help when applying teachable moments to build character. They always took the opportunity to explain why the behavior was wrong when they corrected him. They knew the habits and values they wanted to teach their son based on their son's behavior. They chose consequences that were appropriate to teach that particular value. They taught them to have compassion for strangers by opening doors, saying thank you, or helping someone in need.

STEP – 5: THEY CONTINUALLY WORKED ON MOTIVATING THEM IN ALL AREAS OF THEIR LIFE

They looked to the scripture Joshua 1:9 "Have I not commanded you? Be strong and courageous. Do not be frightened, and do not be dismayed, for the LORD your God is with you wherever you go." They praised and complimented the child's work even if it was less than what they expected. Instead of telling their son how smart they were, they would tell them that their improvements are due to their hard work. They tried to connect their sons with positive Black mentors and role models. This was a huge step. Many of their sons struggled to even imagine what motivation, success, and achievement might look like. They understood Black mentors would help their sons have someone to look up to who looked like them. They might have even wanted to follow in their footsteps. They reached out to coaches, influential teachers, program activity instructors, camp counselors, or a successful family member to help them. These mothers knew having supportive adults involved in their boy's life was invaluable. They did whatever it took to connect their sons to positive, encouraging mentors.

STEP – 6: THEY WOULD TEACH THEM HOW TO VALUE TIME AND PRACTICE PUNCTUALITY

They used the biblical principal of Ephesians 5:15-16 ESV, "Look carefully then how you walk, not as unwise but as wise, making the best use of the time, because the days are evil." This was a principle tied to Step - 3, goal setting.

Most of these moms, used as role models for their sons, people who set goals and wanted to achieve something in life. The majority of these role models valued time because they understood that every second counts if they were going to accomplish their dreams or goals. They taught them something as simple as how to prepare for the upcoming day by getting their clothes and other required items together the night before. They also taught to always show up 15 minutes early in order to plan for any trouble that might occur. Being on time would cause people to see that they were reliable and that they could be trusted to do whatever they said they would do.

STEP 7 – HELP THEM DEVELOP SELF-DISCIPLINE

They followed 2 Timothy 1:7, "For the Spirit God gave us does not make us timid, but gives us power, love and self-discipline." Another word for self-discipline is self-control. The parent used this scripture to teach the child three basic concepts about self-control: (1) to respects the needs of others; (2) to respect authority; and (3) to learn to except results even when it was the not the way they wish it would end. For instance, losing a ball game, not getting a job, or practicing real hard and still not making the team.

Most kids have some form of self-control only because of outward pressures. Without this outward force, they would not do what they do. They do not realize what benefits they gain from having these pressures on their lives. The outward pressures these mothers put on their boy consisted of setting rules that had to be followed or there would be negative consequences if not followed. She gave them daily and weekly tasks to be completed and the level they were to be completed, if not followed again there would be consequences. This was done repetitively and consistently.

These boys had a healthy fear of their mothers. This healthy fear helped shape those boys' thinking because they knew that their moms would apply negative consequences if they did not do what she said. This is how a mother helps mold their son's morals, values, and ethics for a lifetime. The fear really was respect for their mothers. The respect these boys had for their moms kept them doing the right thing and avoiding getting into trouble. These moms brought about consistent training and modeling to the boys so that they learned to obey the rules even when she was not present. As they got older, they began to understand these as the morals and values of their family.

STEP 8 – THEY PLANTED SEEDS OF SUCCESS

These moms invested the time to plant seeds of success in their sons. They created a positive vision of what people can become and continually encouraged and nudged them along that path. These moms taught their sons that they were a child of destiny. They would say, "you are destined for great things." She would provide them with ways to explore their interests by trying new things and finding their passion and purpose in life. They would find out what their son's passion was and who he looked up to in the field . They did this so their sons could have role models as an example to emulate. They would get their son to research and find out how that person made it to the top. They taught their sons that success does not come on a silver platter; you have to work hard for it. Also, they were told you cannot succeed if you procrastinate, so they had to get busy doing it right away.

STEP – 9: THEY TAUGHT THEM GOOD WORK ETHICS

They used 2 Thessalonians 3:10-13, "Don't you remember the rule we had when we lived with you? "If you don't work, you don't eat."

These boys picked up good values of hard work by watching their mother working hard. Mom knew that they dealt with their sons every day, and what they saw all the time becomes a habit, so these moms made sure it was a good habit. They had a strategy for teaching good work ethics.

a. They established limits.
b. They created boundaries that pushed their sons away from distractions and toward his work.
c. They followed up on limits to ensure the boy was following the rule.
d. They would help their sons with their chores and homework, but they did not do it for them.
e. They rewarded their son's productivity.

STEP – 10: THEY TAUGHT THEM GOAL SETTING

They operated from Psalm 20:4 NIV, "May he give you the desire of your heart and make all your plans succeed."

Old school Black Moms, while pointing their sons toward goal setting, understood the first step was to help him recognize the importance of self-belief and self-confidence as early as possible in his development. These moms would help their sons put on paper clear measurable goals. They would help them create action plans for each goal. They got them to visualize themselves accomplishing the goals. She would always have them look at their progress to see if they were on target. The mom would help them revise their action plan when needed. And finally, they would celebrate their accomplishments and successes.

THE BELT

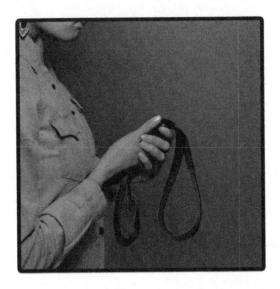

The phrase, "Spare the rod, spoil the child" is often thought to be a proverb from the Bible, but it actually comes from a guy named Samuel Butler in a 1662 poem. However, it is clearly built upon Proverbs 13:24, "Whoever spares the rod hates his son, but he who loves him is diligent to discipline." These old school Black Moms used the analogy of the belt by bringing both words and actions, warnings, and consequences into all situations in their son's life in order to keep him on track.

These Black mother's sons had a healthy fear of them. This fear is understood as ultimate respect for the mother and the type of discipline she gives them throughout this growth and development period. These mothers believed that discipline was about watching their son to see the direction in which he's going. They let the boy make guided decisions. Yet, they would step in when they saw their son taking the wrong route and headed toward destruction. They understood that he probably would get mad for a while when they stepped in, but ten years down the road, he'll thank them. Remember, this anger will not last forever, but destruction, however, just might.

Old school Black Moms knew that one of the most powerful ways to love their child was to be consistent in their discipline. Sometimes, that was really hard. It goes back to the old saying, "This is going to hurt me more than it will hurt you." They were not trying to maintain a friendship, another old saying, "I am not your little friend". They gave them what was best for them, which was discipline with the understanding that they did it out of love. They were integrating this behavior into their personality. Teaching them how to self-discipline themselves rather than having discipline imposed on them all the time. Therefore, they regulated how they spoke, their tone of voice, and how they acted toward other people. This is so it would become a part of who they are so that when they weren't there to regulate their conduct, the acceptable behavior would remain.

These mothers understood that their sons did not like

the discipline that they were imposing. But they knew their sons would love and appreciate them when they looked back on these times years later. They really had to stand their ground, especially when their sons would make statements such as, "What do you mean I'm grounded? I really can't go? I hate you! You're the worst parent in the world!", and "It's like my mom chains me to the bedpost. I never get to go anywhere." They would have to remind themselves that their sons were reaping negative consequences based on their negative actions. Giving in was not an option; even if their kids came back and said they were sorry for their actions, these moms knew that they must teach their sons the concept of cause and effect. Consistency was vital as they had to follow through on their decision to discipline their child. It was tough for these moms to discipline their sons because when they punished their children, they also had to punish themselves. If kids are grounded, someone has to be there to enforce the penalty. Not compromising, no matter how inconvenient, allowed the son to understand that mom meant what she said and showed him that the world has real-life consequences.

IT TAKES A VILLAGE TO RAISE A CHILD

"It takes a village to raise a child" is an African proverb that means that an entire community of people must interact with children for those children to experience and grow in a safe and healthy environment. This community behavior was a part of that "belt" spoken of earlier by bringing both words and actions, warnings, and consequences into all situations in their son's life in order to keep him on track. The concept allowed the community to give boys correction and discipline. I remember when I was a child, if you were misbehaving, the neighbor could correct you by spanking you. The correcting did not stop at that point because they would also call your mom or even come to your house and let your mom know what you had been doing. This proverb was a staple in the Black community in years past. The proverb illustrates the importance African cultures have on family and community. The old school Black Moms understood it took an entire community to raise their children. People in their village fed them, allowed them to spend the night at their homes, watched them as they played in the streets, and even disciplined them.

Many boys today are lonely, stressed out, isolated, and lack the same social skills and social/emotional intelligence because they did not grow up around family, extended family, and other community supports. The existence of the village framework helped raise those boys, with past generations assisting the mom in rearing them to become successful men. Many of today's young men do not have this village framework and only rely on that single mom to guide them during their growth and development period. One person, no matter how hard they may try, cannot raise a child alone. Children learn from parents and their village how to interact with the world around them, including how to adapt to a changing society.

The village helped those old school Black Moms to raise their boys in a safe and healthy environment which instilled/included the following:

a. How to show love and gratitude for the family.
b. How to make both the boys and the moms accountable for their behavior.
c. For many latchkey boys, it reduced loneliness, isolation, and built confidence.
d. Taught and reinforced healthy boundaries.
e. How to show love and respect for others.
f. Provided the opportunity to spend quality time with adult community members.
g. How to communicate their feelings.

    h. Provided love and support outside of the home.
    i. Helped keep the boys safe.
    j. How to become self-disciplined/self-controlled.
    k. Inspired them to work hard so the community would be proud of their future successes.

These boys did not come with instruction manuals because every one of them were different. The village consisted of having a strong support system that included experienced elders and surrogate parents who offered support and guidance, who showed them how to become positive productive young men. A good village can provide children with the tools, skills, and eyes/ears parents do not always have. There is no such thing as pulling yourself up by your bootstraps. We need each other to survive, no matter how much our government and politicians tell us otherwise.

WHAT HAPPENED TO THE VILLAGE?

Because many of the moms of today were not raised in the village, they think they need to do everything by themselves. This type of behavior may explain why they are now more stressed, their sons lack social skills, are more likely to be depressed, and get into more trouble. The communities they live in are less safe, and their life spans are shorter.

When the village attempts to help raise their children, they become very defensive. Often, when you tell them that their child is doing something wrong, they respond with something similar to, "who are you to tell me how to raise my child!" Whereas in the past, if you were a part of the village and its members came and told you that your child was misbehaving, you would likely be receptive to the information. Most old school Black Moms even allowed those village members to chastise their children when they were found doing something wrong.

These new-school Black moms need our help to survive and teach their sons how to become men. These mothers must be taught that when they rely on family, friends, and community members to help with their children's growth and development, both they and their sons are better for it. Because these mothers isolate their sons from extended family and the community at-large, their spiritual, mental, and emotional growth go lacking.

If you were blessed to be raised with a village framework of good, loving people, with good intentions, then you know the value of a good village. These new-breed moms would benefit from understanding that people in the community can help monitor their children when they are not around. For the village framework to work, these new-school Black Moms must transform their minds to a village mindset. They must understand that they need others to help with their children, so they must relinquish some of their control and inform their children that the village will be helping to raise them. Village frameworks will not work where parents undermine the village. By undermining the village, parents teach children that there is always a back door, and they don't have to listen to anyone except the parents. That line of thinking ends up being a huge problem by the time the child reaches adulthood.

1. The church should be a part of the village framework. Church members can keep an eye on your children and can report when they are misbehaving. The church can ensure your son doesn't make any wrong moves. There is no "I," "me," or "my" in the village. The village kids are our kids.

2. Coaches from teams your son plays on should be a part of the village framework. They can help by telling you about your son's potential and advise if there is a need to go in a different direction.

3. Male friends, uncles, granddads, ex-boyfriends, and other male acquaintances in your life should be a part of the village framework. They can pour into your son's life, by guiding him toward manhood.

4. Community members should be a part of the village framework. When your son is in the neighborhood acting any other way besides "the right way," community members will correct them immediately on the spot. Other community members that can be a

member of the village framework could be the barber, corner store owner, or the senior citizen sitting on the back porch.

5. These old school Black Moms surrounded their boys with community members who were dedicated not only to helping Black Boys become awesome successful young men, but assuring that they lived and grew in a safe and healthy environment.

About the Author

Dr. Calvin Avant is a native of Pensacola, Florida, and is a product of the Escambia County Public School System. Dr. Avant is the retired Executive Director of the Escambia Pensacola Human Relations Commission. Dr. Avant is a veteran of the U. S. Navy. His academic accomplishments include a Bachelor of Science in Education from the University of West Florida, a Master of Arts in Management and Leadership from Webster University, and a Doctor of Ministry of Psychology from Faith Bible Theological Seminary. Dr. Avant is a widower and the father of one daughter, Amy.

Dr. Avant is a Certified State of Florida School Teacher in Physical Education, Special Ed. and Elementary Ed., a Certified After Care Specialist, a Certified Parent Instructor, a Licensed Addiction Counselor, a Certified Florida Supreme Court Mediator, a State Endorse for Prison Ministry Training, and National Validator for Before and After Schools Programs. As Executive Director of Unity in the Family Ministry, Dr. Avant, in collaboration with the Deep South Center for Environmental Justice (D.S.C.E.J.) in New Orleans, LA, conducts an environmental remediation training program entitled Environmental Career Worker Training Program. In partnership with D.S.C.E.J., he also manages an Environmental Justice Project entitled HBCU-CBO Equity Consortium, and a Digital Storytelling Project concerning targeted environmental justice communities in Pensacola, FL, with three high school students as interns. Also, he operates a grant-funded summer program entitled Environmental Justice Youth Exposed to S.T.E.M.M. for students who are in the fourth and fifth grades. Dr. Avant is an ordained minister and pastor of Unity in the Family Ministry.

Publications
- "So, You Are Raising a Knuckle Head" – Parenting Curriculum
- "Reinvent Yourself with Dr. Calvin Avant" – Poems and Prose
- "Better Way Substance Abuse Training Manual"
- "Youth Exposed to Success, Y.E.S. Program" – Elementary School Social Skill Curriculum
- "Teens Altering Behavior of Self, T.A.B.S. Program" – Teen Social Skill Manual
- "It's Just Prison Telling Teens the Real Deal"

Additional Information: Scholastic Performance
- University District of Columbia Certified Addiction Aftercare Specialist
- Center for Improvement of Child Care Certified Parenting Instructor
- Faith Temple Christian Center Ordained/License Evangelist and Elder
- Prison Fellowship Ministry State Endorse for Prison Ministry Trainer

References

Williams, R. (2014). The Decline of Fatherhood and the Male Identity Crisis. Psychology Today. https://www.psychologytoday.com/blog/wired-success/201406/the-male-identity-crisis-and-the-decline-fatherhood

McLanahan, S., & Jencks, C. (2015). Was Moynihan Right? What happens to the children of unmarried mothers. Education Next. https://www.educationnext.org/was-moynihan-right/

Ellis, C. (2009). Growing up without father: the effects on African American boys. MINDS@UW. https://minds.wisconsin.edu/handle/1793/38560

Fouzder, M. (2016). Minority defendants more likely to plead "not guilty." Law Gazette. https://www.lawgazette.co.uk/law/minority-defendants-more-likely-to-plead-not-guilty/5058811.article

Livingston, G. (2018). The changing profile of unmarried parents. Pew Research Center's Social & Demographic Trends Project. https://www.pewsocialtrends.org/2018/04/25/the-changing-profile-of-unmarried-parents/

Meyer, C. (2018). Parental alienation: Do you know these 6 signs?. LiveAbout. https://www.liveabout.com/signs-of-parental-alienation-syndrome-1103082

Joiner, L. (2016). Hurt: The impact of father-absence on the mental health of black boys. USC Center for Health Journalism. https://centerforhealthjournalism.org/our-work/reporting/hurt-impact-father-absence-mental-health-black-boys

Lehman, J. (n.d.). Your child is not your friend. Empowering Parents. https://www.empoweringparents.com/article/your-child-is-not-your-friend/

The Right Step. (2017). Psychological effects of covert incest. https://www.rightstep.com/rehab-blog/psychological-effects-covert-incest/

blackleaderanalysis. (2016). Black Mothers, Black Sons, and Enmeshment. Black Leadership Analysis. https://blackleaderanalysis.com/tag/parenting/

Burney, R. (n.d.). Emotional Incest - Emotionally Devastating Child Abuse. Dance of Wounded Souls. https://www.danceofwoundedsouls.com/emotional-incest

Weber, E. (2009). Move Intelligence Up a Notch Today. Brain Leaders And Learners. https://brainleadersandlearners.com/?p=154

Hester, N., & Gray, K. (2018). For Black men, Being Tall Increases Threat Stereotyping and Police Stops. PNAS. https://www.pnas.org/doi/10.1073/pnas.1714454115

Harris, A. (2021). The Burden of Being "On Point." The Atlantic. https://www.theatlantic.com/politics/archive/2021/04/black-boys-trauma-misunderstood-behavior/618684/

Goff, P. A. (2014). Black Boys Viewed as Older, Less Innocent than Whites, Research Finds. American Psychological Association. https://www.apa.org/news/press/releases/2014/03/black-boys-older

Harpalani, V. (2017). Counterstereotypic Identity Among High-

Achieving Black Students. 14(1) Perspectives on Urban Education, Available at SSRN: https://ssrn.com/abstract=3153154

Dutro, E., & Bien, A. C. (2014). Listening to the speaking wound. American Educational Research Journal, 51(1), 7–35. https://doi.org/10.3102/0002831213503181

Solis, G. (2021). For Black Parents, 'The Talk' Binds Benerations, Reflects Changes in America. USC Today. https://today.usc.edu/the-talk-usc-black-parents-children-racism-america/

Know Your rights: Police Interactions for Black and Brown People: ACLU of Northern California. ACLU of Northern California. (2020). https://www.aclunc.org/our-work/know-your-rights/know-your-rights-police-interactions-black-and-brown-people

Know Your Rights: Stopped By Police: ACLU. American Civil Liberties Union. (2023). https://www.aclu.org/know-your-rights/stopped-by-police?redirect=files%2Fkyr%2Fkyr_english.pdf

Wire, T. E. (2021). Responsibilities of Black Fathers Have Increased in the Face of Racism. Afrik Digest. https://www.afrikdigest.com/responsibilities-of-black-fathers-have-increased-in-the-face-of-racism-by-trice-edney-wire/

Okeke-Adeyanju, N., Taylor, L. C., Craig, A. B., Smith, R. E., Thomas, A., Boyle, A. E., & DeRosier, M. E. (2014). Celebrating the strengths of black youth: Increasing self-esteem and implications for prevention. The journal of primary prevention. https://www.ncbi.nlm.nih.gov/pmc/articles/PMC4152398/#R27

Gershenson, S., Hart, C. M. D., Lindsay, C. A., & Papageorge, N. W. (2017). The Long-Run Impacts of Same-Race Teachers. IZA. https://www.iza.org/publications/dp/10630

Hobbs, W. (2020). "I Become What I See": Addressing Academic Patterning Distress and the Importance of Black Male Teachers. UNCF. https://uncf.org/the-latest/i-become-what-i-see-addressing-academic-patterning-distress-and-the-importance-of-black-male-teachers

Wright, B. L. (2019). Black Boys Matter: Strategies for a Culturally Responsive Classroom. NAEYC. https://www.naeyc.org/resources/pubs/tyc/apr2019/strategies-culturally-responsive-classroom

Pollard, N. (2020). Student Voice: Why we Need More Teachers Who Are Black Men. The Hechinger Report. https://hechingerreport.org/student-voice-black-boys-need-the-guidance-and-mentorship-of-black-male-teachers/

Fink, J. L. W. (2018). How to Build Up Black Boys. Breaking Barriers. https://www.breakingbarriersbuffalo.org/post/how-to-build-up-black-boys

Mader, J. (2019). Too Few Parents Talking to Kids About Race and Identity, Report Finds. The Hechinger Report. https://hechingerreport.org/too-few-parents-talk-to-their-kids-about-race-and-identity-report-finds/

Terry, D. (1994). Basketball at Midnight: "Hope" on a Summer Eve. The New York Times. https://www.nytimes.com/1994/08/19/us/basketball-at-midnight-hope-on-a-summer-eve.html

Hartmann, D., & Depro, B. (2006). Rethinking sports-based

Community Crime Prevention. Journal of Sport and Social Issues, 30(2), 180–196. https://doi.org/10.1177/0193723506286863

Still, B. (2013). Individual Characteristics, Protective Factors and Processes Significant in Helping Low-Income African American Students Achieve Academic Success and Projected Upward Mobility. https://core.ac.uk/download/234122645.pdf

Will, M. (2019). 65 Years After "Brown v. Board," Where Are All the Black Educators? Education Week. https://www.edweek.org/policy-politics/65-years-after-brown-v-board-where-are-all-the-black-educators/2019/05?r=787874109